Breaking the Chains
The Empowerment of Employees

How to Evaluate, Monitor, and Improve Employee Empowerment Levels

Allen J. Klose

Continental Business Books

Copyright © 1993 by Allen J. Klose

Published by Continental Business Books, 3800 Old Cheney Road, Suite #101-103 Lincoln, NE 68516.

Publisher's Cataloging in Publication
(Prepared by Quality Books Inc.)

Klose, Allen J.
    Breaking the chains : the empowerment of employees : how to evaluate, monitor, and improve employee empowerment levels / Allen J. Klose.
    p. cm.
    Includes bibliographical references.
    Preassigned LCCN: 93-72789.
    ISBN 0-9637927-9-2
    1. Organizational effectiveness. 2. Organizational change. 3. Job enrichment. I. Title.

HD58.9.K56 1993   658.3'14
                             QBI93-1217

To Jacqueline,

whose love and encouragement
empowered me to continue writing.

Contents

Contents (cont.)

Page

Introduction

**You can hear it from the factory floors,
in office building corridors,
and even from a delivery truck's door -**

"The employees are being set free."

For many American businesses, the days of the autocratic manager and the subservient employee are no longer appropriate. International competition has eroded away domestic market share and pushed many U.S. businesses into the red. Corporations are being forced to utilize all their resources efficiently and effectively, including the creative abilities of their employees. In short, U.S. businesses are being forced to break the chains and empower their employees.

The process of moving to this new style of management has been referred to as a paradigm shift. Management styles concerned with order and control are being replaced by a style based on participation, achieving results, and collaboration. [1] Driven by a need to be adaptive and to customize products and services, organizations across the country are producing a new breed of manager. Product manufacturers see increased employee participation as a way to improve productivity, reduce costs and produce higher quality products. Service organizations view employee empowerment as the mechanism allowing them the ability to adapt and customize themselves to every potential customer.

Preliminary research indicates a great opportunity for improvement with this new style of management. Employee empowerment programs have the opportunity to unleash a tremendous amount of creativity and energy stored within employees. Over 75% of the employees surveyed in one study indicated they could be more effective in their job's than they are now, and fewer than 25% of the employees said they were currently working at their full potential. [2] Just think of the opportunities!

Every manager has the opportunity to capitalize on the energy stored within his or her employees. This book will trace employee empowerment from its theoretical roots to present day business examples, demonstrate how it can be measured, outline the process of becoming an organizational emancipator, and present many of the myths circulating about this subject.

"An empowered employee will be ready to do battle."

Part I Employee Empowerment

Employee Empowerment

The employees were gathered all snug in the room,
waiting for their boss and a proclamation of doom;

But this time it was different as he spoke from the stand,
"Lets all work together by lending a hand";

"You'll all have control over your work and decisions,
these changes are part of the organizational mission";

Empowerment was the word he used when he spoke,
a saviorlike theory it wasn't a joke;

However, when he finished they all looked around,
the new empowered spirit was nowhere to be found;

"How could this be, he spoke for an hour,
sharing with the employees and giving them power";

Yet the employees felt nothing as this book will show,
empowerment is much more and it takes time to grow.

"Now go back to work and BE EMPOWERED!"

Chapter 1 Employee Empowerment

Why study employee empowerment?

The study of employee empowerment is important for two reasons. First, organizations depend on responsible and capable employees to operate effectively. Businesses are under pressure from consumers and investors to provide high quality products and services. Employee empowerment programs have been shown to be one way to achieve these goals.

Second, employee empowerment is a complex subject. Reading a magazine article or attending a half-day seminar on employee empowerment is not enough to learn all that is important. There are several components to employee empowerment, all of which must be understood before an effective employee empowerment program can be developed.

Background

The idea of empowerment has been around for hundreds of years. First used as a legal term for granting authority, empowerment has evolved into a term with many uses and meanings.

Current interpretations of empowerment began to surface in the 1960's. Sociologists of this time period referred to empowerment as a motivating factor that would help minorities rise above their poverty. Empowerment was seen as a force that would deliver this depressed segment of the population from its problems.

During the 1960's, empowerment was seen as the answer to some critical societal problems. The Civil Rights Movement and its legions of press insured that the idea of "minority" empowerment reached the American public.

Shortly thereafter, the use of the term empowerment emerged with management practitioners. While many of the concepts associated with **employee empowerment** can be traced back to much earlier dates (see Table 1: Evolution of Concepts Associated with Employee Empowerment), it was not until the mid-1970's when management practitioners began to use the term empowerment in the business setting.

Today, most business publications are overflowing with examples of the employee empowerment process. It is clear from all this information, managers and businesses across the country are now talking about and using many of the principles of employee empowerment.

→ Pacific Gas and Electric's policy of listening to employee suggestions has resulted in substantial savings. "Employee suggestions have enabled the company to lay almost three times as much cable, without an increase in workers, at only about a third the cost per foot." [6]

→ In recent Forbes interview, American Express's John Robinson III said, "The problem with excessive autocracy is that it breeds mediocrity down and through the corporation. The more participatory you are, the more people have a chance to be full and aggressive team members." [7]

→ "At Minnesota's Shott Transformers time clocks were removed. Employees were made responsible for their own work hours as long as customer service and productivity were not effected." [8]

→ Federal Express uses several means to empower employees. One of their most successful is an interactive video training system that allows employees to learn at their own pace. According one Federal Express executive, "the best possible customer service comes from employees who are well trained and knowledgeable." [9]

Table 1.

Evolution of Concepts Associated with Employee Empowerment

1933 - Elton Mayo spoke out against the authoritarian practices of management. [1]

1937 - H. H. Carey refers to "Consulting Supervision," a participative approach to management. [2]

1950 - George Homans began looking at how the interrelationships and interactions between individuals and between work groups affect organizational performance. [3]

1959 - Frederick Herzberg discusses the difference between Hygiene Factors and Real Motivators.

Hygiene Factors are items such as pay, working conditions, hours, etc.

Real Motivators are items such as increased responsibility, challenge, recognition, etc.

Herzberg considered the Real Motivators to be the key to improving worker performance. [4]

1960 - Douglas McGregor developed his Theory X - Theory Y.

Theory X - Man is lazy and needs supervision.

Theory Y - Man seeks responsibility and is capable of self-control. [5]

→   Herman Maass at General Motors' Buick City Plant says that quality is improved by "giving people--particularly hourly workers--the encouragement to share ideas and acting on what they suggest." [10]

→   At Southwestern Bell, Zane Barnes was quoted as saying, "My personal view of power is that it's my job as a chief executive officer to empower those around me." [11]

→   The Ford Taurus Plant in Atlanta uses a process of involving its front line employees. "When complaints and suggestions come in from customers, they are routed to the appropriate workers. When those workers suggest solutions to problems, management listens." [12]

→   "Many new plants in the United States that have been designed to maximize employee involvement have utilized the work team model: TRW, Digital Equipment, Proctor and Gamble, and Johnson and Johnson have built plants with teams." [13]

→   "Today more than 20% of GE's 120,000 employees work under a team concept." [14]

After reading these statements it is clear the idea of employee empowerment has evoked interest with managers and the business community. While many of these organizations and individuals have found different ways to empower their employees, the general concept of employee empowerment has taken hold as an organizational efficiency issue.

In addition to the many examples of employee empowerment, nearly an equal number of statements define employee empowerment. This vast variety of definitions poses a critical problem for the development of meaningful dialogue on the subject. As with any concept or idea, there is a need for a solid definition. Without a solid definition it is very difficult to gain an understanding and communicate an idea.

Empowerment Defined

Developing a solid definition for employee empowerment is not an easy task. It seems that virtually every consultant in America has a different idea about what employee empowerment is. As a result of this diversity, articles and books written on this subject have very little consistency.

Employee empowerment is defined by some as a relational concept. Empowering employees implies granting them more authority.

> **"To empower, implies the granting of power--delegation of authority."** [15]

To the relational group an employee can be empowered simply by increasing their level of responsibility. "Empowerment is obtained by pushing power down the corporate pyramid." [16]

Others define employee empowerment as a motivational concept. Employees are empowered by enhancing their feelings of personal efficacy. (Personal efficacy is the level of empowerment individual's feel in their lives.)

> **"A process of enhancing feelings of self-efficacy among organizational members through the identification of conditions that foster powerlessness and through their removal by both formal and organizational practices and informal techniques of providing efficacy information."** [17]

Still another group defines employee empowerment by indicating a list of specific things that empowered employees should be able to do.

> "Empowerment involves giving employees the flexibility to use their judgment in serving customers, training to support their judgment, and a sense of ownership in the customer satisfaction mission..." [18]

As will become apparent later in this book, the definition of employee empowerment is critical. Employee empowerment's definition will determine how it is measured and what can be said about it.

In addition, the definition must make it unique from other concepts. For example, if employee empowerment is nothing more than the sharing of power, then the concept needs no more analysis or definition beyond that of power.

The definition must also be practical and understandable. If the concept is defined in such a manner that its operationalization becomes impractical, then the concept is worthless. Organizations and managers are not interested in a concept that cannot be easily related and measured in the real world.

The same can be said for concepts that are not easily understandable. A concept that cannot be easily understood will have limited value. Mutual understanding is a requirement of all communication. And without understanding, the level of communication required to utilize a concept effectively cannot be achieved.

Bridging the conceptual gaps created by these earlier employee empowerment writers is not an easy task. A new universal employee empowerment definition must maintain the flavor of what has gone before. Employee empowerment's definition must be generic enough to apply to varied workplaces, yet structured enough to be clear and concise.

After a myriad of discussions and revisions, the following definition emerged:

> **Employee empowerment** is the degree to which employees feel they can be both proactive and reactive to the situations surrounding their job.

> **Empowering employees** is the process in which employees are brought to feel they can be both proactive and reactive to the situations surrounding their job.

Employee empowerment is a FEELING

It is important to note employee empowerment is defined as a feeling. Changing an employee's level of empowerment requires changing the way an employee feels about work.

There are many tangible and visual processes claiming to improve employee empowerment. However, if they have no effect on the way the employee feels, then they will also have no effect on the employee's level of empowerment. If a training program is not designed to change the way an employee feels, then the training program will not increase an employee's empowerment levels.

When selecting or developing an employee empowerment program, it is important to consider the components of employee empowerment (see Chapter 2). Employee empowerment programs must be targeted at these components. If employee empowerment programs do not contain these components they cannot be called employee empowerment programs.

Employee empowerment is not the same as power

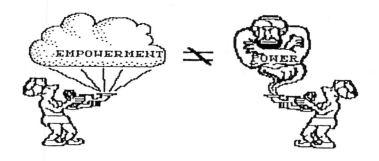

While it may be easy to think of employee empowerment and power as being the same, they are not. The definition of employee empowerment has been carefully developed to ensure it is unique from all other concepts. Part of the validation process for any concept is to establish theoretical uniqueness.

If employee empowerment were the same as another concept such as power, there would be no reason to study employee empowerment. One could learn everything about employee empowerment simply by reading about power.

Employee empowerment and power are terms describing two different concepts. And like employee empowerment, the concept of power has many definitions. Yet, for the purpose of this book, power is described as an implied concept. Power is defined as what is implied by an employee's status within an organization.

An employee's power is the authority and ability implied by their position in an organization. French and Raven refer to this type of power as "Legitimate and Expert Power." [19]

Every employee has a certain level of power based on the authority and ability implied by their position in an organization. "Legitimate Power comes from the position of a superior in the organizational hierarchy and Expert Power resides with an individual with an expertise, special skill, or knowledge". [20]

The implied nature of power is very different from employee empowerment. Employee empowerment is a concept that relates to an employee's actual feeling. It is a concept which looks at whether an employee actually feels authorized or enabled.

Power
Implied Authority

Implied Ability

Empowerment
Authorized

Enabled

An employee's level of empowerment may or may not have any relationship to an employee's status or level in an organization. A supervisor's position implies more power than the subordinate; however, it is very possible for a supervisor to feel less empowered than their subordinates.

An employee's training is also not a guarantee of the empowerment level. While expert authority may give the employee a tremendous feeling of power, there are still several reasons why an employee may not feel empowered. A very simple example of this situation is an organization with a communication problem. In this case, an employee can have all the expert authority in the world, yet if no communication system is in place for ideas to be expressed, feelings of empowerment will be very low.

As is mentioned with Myth 2 later in this book, employee empowerment programs may need to be designed for all levels of an organization. It is dangerous to assume that because managers have power they will also feel empowered.

Let the employees go free

Even before Moses lead the Israelites out of Egypt, people have strived to be free. Over the years, millions have fled from tyranny and fought for control of their lives. Led by great emancipators, the human race has yearned to be free.

It is generally agreed that organizations are better off with employees who feel empowered. Establishing the empowered feeling, however, is not an easy task. An employee's feeling of empowerment is a complex subject and deserves careful review. The next chapter of this book looks at the use of an employee empowerment measuring tool.

Measuring current levels of employee empowerment is the first step in determining an organization's status. Once an organization's status is known, appropriate empowerment techniques can be developed and employed. Measuring current levels may even reveal very high levels of employee empowerment. If this is the case, additional training and empowerment programs may be ineffective at raising employee empowerment levels further.

Chapter 2   Measuring the Feeling of Empowerment Among Employees

"Measure it--or forget it!"

James A. Belasco, Ph.D.,
Teaching the Elephant to Dance

The process of surveying employees has been used in American business for nearly 40 years. During this time an increasing number of businesses have discovered the value of obtaining employee input. Employees have been asked to evaluate working conditions, pay, benefits, training, communication, job satisfaction, etc. If fact, just about anything a business needs to know about its employees has been covered in some form of employee survey.

Measuring an employee's feeling of empowerment is no exception. Using the specially designed survey presented in Figure 1, it is possible to measure the feeling of empowerment employees have with their jobs. (William Byham, in his book, Zapp! The Lightning of Empowerment, refers to a tool used to measure employee empowerment levels as a **Zappometer.** [1]) In addition to measuring individual levels of empowerment, it is possible to assess the varying levels of empowerment between employees, between the various departments within an organization, and to track empowerment levels as they change over time.

Determine Need

Implementing the employee empowerment survey should be the first step in your organization's empowerment plan. The results of an initial round of empowerment surveys will pinpoint the empowerment needs of your organization. This situational assessment will help you evaluate the needs within your organization and determine what should be done to empower your employees.

While conducting this situational assessment, it will be necessary for you to answer a few questions. Your answers to each of these questions will help to shape the strategy your organization develops for improving employee empowerment levels.

→ **How empowered do our employees feel?**

→ **Do empowerment levels differ greatly within the departments in our organization?**

→ **Do empowerment levels differ greatly throughout our organization?**

→ **Do our managers have different levels of empowerment than our front line employees?**

→ **Can we develop the specific programs necessary to improve empowerment among our employees?**

→ **If empowerment levels are high, how will this change our strategy of increasing employee involvement?**

There are no right or wrong answers to these questions. However, without answers, it will be very difficult to develop an effective empowerment program. The success of your empowerment program will hinge on the answers you give to these questions and the empowerment strategy you develop because of these answers.

Empowerment Strategy

Because employee empowerment is a means to some greater end (i.e., increasing organizational efficiency to lower operating costs, improving product quality and enhancing corporate profits, encouraging innovation and capturing higher portions of market share, etc.), it is essential to determine current levels of employee empowerment so that you can develop an appropriate empowerment strategy. Employee empowerment is measured given the current constraints and freedoms surrounding an employee's job. Changing the situations involved with an employee's job without taking into consideration the employees level of empowerment could have adverse effects on the employee's empowerment level.

For example: Employees who have high feelings of empowerment may actually have these feelings lowered if additional responsibilities and pressures are added to their job. In this case, training may be required to ensure that empowerment levels are maintained as an employee's responsibilities are increased.

While working with a service organization in the Midwest, a situation like this arose. The management of this company was looking to expand the responsibilities of the receptionist. The receptionist was responsible for answering the telephone and offering assistance and directions to customers visiting the company. With these limited responsibilities the receptionist had a very high feeling of empowerment. She was able to handle all situations and make the necessary decisions required for her position.

The managers, however, wanted to increase the receptionist's responsibilities. In addition to her current responsibilities, they wanted her to begin taking messages and typing correspondence for some of the members of the company. What the managers failed to consider was how these additional responsibilities would impact the receptionist's feeling of empowerment.

While the receptionist had received extensive training in phone answering skills and customer service, she had never received training in shorthand or word processing. Without these additional skills it was very difficult for her to manage these new tasks. In fact, a few days after these additional responsibilities were added to her job, the quality of her phone service began to decline. Calls were ringing seven and eight times before they were answered, people were left on hold, and messages were being lost.

Before long, customer complaints began to reach management. Shocked and angered by these service complaints, the managers stormed down the receptionist's desk and demanded an explanation.

The receptionist, almost in tears, exclaimed that she couldn't handle all of her new responsibilities. "It seems as soon as I begin taking a message, another call comes in. I don't have enough time to transcribe the message without putting someone on hold, or letting the phone ring. And as far as typing correspondence, I am still trying to figure out how to use the word processor."

One of the managers then asked why she hadn't told them of her problems. Her response was that she was worried about being fired.

In this situation, the managers added responsibilities without first looking at qualifications. While it is important to allow your employees the opportunity to grow, it is also important not to throw them in over their heads. Giving employees too much responsibility too soon can be counterproductive and can actually decrease their empowerment levels. Therefore, it is essential to determine the qualifications of your employees first and then you will be able to add responsibilities at an appropriate and productive pace.

It is also very possible that you will find employees with low feelings of empowerment. Once again, before you can develop a strategy to increase these empowerment levels, it will be necessary to find out why these feelings of empowerment are low.

For example, you may find one group of employees whose feelings of empowerment are low because of a lack of training, and another group whose feelings of empowerment are low because of an inability to use their training and skills on the job. In this example, it is clear that an empowerment program which focused solely on training would be inappropriate to one group of employees, and an empowerment program focusing solely on increasing the responsibilities of employees would be inappropriate to the other group.

Therefore, to solve this problem, you must develop an empowerment strategy which consists of two components. For the first group of employees, you will need to develop an appropriate training program or series of training programs. A properly developed training program will help ensure that this group becomes better able to complete their jobs. Increasing job competency should result in their increased empowerment levels.

As for the second group, you will need to look specifically at the employees and their positions. For some of these employees, it may be possible to increase responsibilities. If this can be done, it will help ensure that their jobs become more challenging and that their empowerment levels rise. However, if it is not possible to increase an employees responsibilities, it may then be necessary to reassign the employee into more challenging position. Reassigning employees into more challenging positions will allow employees to grow, thus increasing their levels of empowerment.

These are only two examples of how an empowerment strategy might be influenced by the empowerment levels of your employees. You may have to consider these and several others to facilitate an effective change in your organization. Your empowerment strategy might include the development of more effective communication channels, training, providing employees with more decision-making authority, adding additional responsibilities where necessary, improving facilities, allowing employees more time to do their job, the purchase of state-of-the-art equipment, the enhancement of a sense of commitment among employees, etc. However, before your strategy can be developed, you must measure the empowerment levels of your employees.

Implementing Tool

The first step in measuring your employees' feelings of empowerment is to implement the empowerment survey. The empowerment survey presented in Figure 1 is a paper-and-pencil type questionnaire. The survey is designed to be filled out by an employee in private. The survey can either be administered on-site at your company or it can be sent to the employee's home.

There are benefits and drawbacks to both of these survey administration techniques. The mail survey is typically the least expensive to administer. The mail survey does not require the employee to take time off from work and therefore, results in no company down time. The mail survey does, however, receive a lower response rate. Even though employees are a vested interest group (i.e., they have a vested interest in the results of the survey), obtaining a greater than 75% response is difficult.

On the other hand, the on-site administration, while costing more to conduct, will usually receive the responses of 95% or more of the employees. The on-site administration also ensures that an employee is free from distractions while completing the survey. When an employee completes a survey at home, it is hard to ensure that family members do not assist with the completion of the survey and that the employee remains focused on the questions.

Whichever way you decide to administer the survey, it is important to implement the survey consistently. Use the same administration techniques for collecting all surveys. If you send some out in the mail, send them all out in the mail. Different survey collection techniques may alter the results of your study.

Figure 1.

EMPLOYEE SURVEY

Please respond to each of the following questions in the survey. Your answers will be completely confidential. No one from your organization will see this survey.

Please indicate your level of agreement or disagreement with each of the following statements by circling the appropriate number.

		Strongly Agree	Agree	Undecided	Disagree	Strongly Disagree
1.	My organization limits my opportunity to use my abilities and training on the job. (-)	5	4	3	2	1
2.	I have pressure associated with my job because I am not allowed to make decisions. (-)	5	4	3	2	1
3.	I am able to deal with new problems on my job.	5	4	3	2	1
4.	I have plenty of freedom on the job to use my own judgement.	5	4	3	2	1
5.	I have the necessary resources to try new approaches on my job.	5	4	3	2	1
6.	My manager encourages me to incorporate ideas that will enable me to do my job more effectively and efficiently.	5	4	3	2	1
7.	Management keeps me in the dark about things I ought to know. (-)	5	4	3	2	1
8.	On my job, I seldom get a chance to do things I am trained for. (-)	5	4	3	2	1
9.	I have a lot of freedom to decide how to do my work.	5	4	3	2	1
10.	The other employees in this organization pay no attention to my suggestions. (-)	5	4	3	2	1
11.	I am constantly asking my supervisor for approval on things I am qualified to decide. (-)	5	4	3	2	1
12.	I have little or no control over problems that arise on the job. (-)	5	4	3	2	1
13.	I have all the training and skills necessary to do my job.	5	4	3	2	1
14.	I wish more of my ideas were listened to by management. (-)	5	4	3	2	1

Thank you for taking the time to complete this survey.

It is also important to use the same survey administration techniques over time. If you use an on-site administration technique the first time you measure empowerment levels, be sure to use the on-site technique for future administrations. Altering the way you administer the survey will make it difficult to analyze trends and track change.

Anonymity

One the biggest issues concerning the administration of the empowerment survey is the anonymity of the survey respondent. While guaranteeing anonymity is usually a primary concern with employee surveys, the empowerment survey works the best when you know who the respondents are. When you are able to pinpoint the needs of employees on a personal basis, empowerment strategies can be tailored on an individual basis.

However, encouraging employees to sign their survey is not a simple procedure. Many employees are leery of signing their name to anything, and rightfully so. Many mangers have used employee surveys as means of pinpointing organizational trouble makers (and we all know what happens to trouble makers). Therefore, obtaining employee participation with the empowerment survey, on a personalized basis, will take some time.

The first phase in obtaining the personalized participation of employees, is to build trust. In order to build trust, you must demonstrate that the empowerment survey is designed to help employees and not to hurt them. To do this, you should allow employees to respond anonymously the first time they complete the empowerment survey. Upon the completion of this first round of surveys, you should then present the results to the employees, explaining how the information is being used. Demonstrating and communicating the constructive nature of the survey responses is a critical step in building trust with employees.

When you are ready for the second round of surveys, you can then offer employees the option of signing their names to their survey. When doing this, you must be sure to explain that the personalization is necessary to ensure that each employee receives an empowerment strategy appropriate to them. By this time, you may have acquired the trust of several of the employees, and many will sign their names. With those who have signed their names, it will then be possible to begin personalized empowerment programs.

Once employees commit to signing their names to the empowerment surveys you can also begin providing them with personalized reports displaying their empowerment levels. The personalized report like the one presented in Figure 2 will help employees begin to understand what their empowerment levels mean. The personalized report provides an evaluation of the individual employee empowerment levels and compares this with the others in their department and throughout the organization.

As you continue with the survey process, each time more and more employees should be encouraged to sign their names. After you have completed the third or fourth survey, you will then be ready to sit down with the group of employees who have not been signing their names. Before getting too deep into the empowerment process, it is important to find out why this group is opposed to the empowerment process. By holding a series of small focus groups (approximately 8 - 12 employees), you can attempt to find out what can be done to establish trust with these employees. The overall empowerment of your organization will be limited by the individuals who are opposed to the process. Therefore, it is imperative that everyone be convinced about the importance of the program.

Gaining the commitment of employees through the empowerment survey will help to empower your organization. As employees begin to see organizational changes take place and their empowerment levels rise, their effectiveness and productivity will also increase. Listening to employees is the first step toward involving employees in the decision-making process of your organization.

Figure 2.

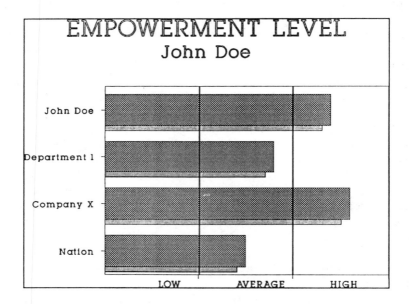

SCORING

HIGH

Yes, you are an empowered employee. You have more of an empowered feeling about your work than do 90% of your fellow employees. Your attitude is what makes your company successful. You have the necessary authority to make a difference and to influence others.

Keep up the good work, it is employees like you that make a difference.

_____

Positive/Negative Questions

When looking at the employee empowerment survey (Figure 1), you will notice that about half of the questions have been written to solicit a negative response. Therefore, before analyzing the data from the employee empowerment surveys, it is important to reverse the scoring on these negative questions. A simple computer program can be written to complete this process. If you fail to reverse the scoring on the negative questions you will receive an inaccurate interpretation of the data.

To make it easy to identify the questions which are to be scored negatively, a (-) has been placed after the appropriate questions. These negative signs have been placed on the survey for your information only. When implementing the survey, it is important to remove these negative signs so they don't influence the respondents.

Scoring

After correcting for the negative questions, scoring of the employe empowerment survey is quite easy. In fact, it is as easy as adding up the responses to each of the questions. (Remember, a score of 1 on a negative (-) question translates into a 5 for scoring purposes.) You will notice that the maximum score an employee can receive on the empowerment survey is 70. A score of 70 would be obtained if an employee received a 5 on all 14 questions. The lowest possible score an employee can receive is 14. A score of 14 is obtained when an employee receives a 1 on all 14 questions. (Another scoring method using standardized scores has been developed; however, for the sake of simplicity, it is not given here.)

To help you understand and interpret the employee empowerment scores, a scoring key is provided in Figure 3. The scoring key was derived from the results of a national sample of employees who completed the empowerment surveys. The region labeled as LOW consists of the scores that are one standard deviation or more below

Figure 3.

Scoring Key

14 to 45   LOW

You have a very low level of empowerment. You feel that you lack authority on your job; you have little or no ability to influence the situations surrounding your job; you cannot make a difference in your organization; and you lack the resources necessary to do your job.

As an unempowered employee, you should sit down with your supervisor to discuss your job and your work environment. You must become more empowered or your work will be unfulfilling for both you and to your company.

46 to 58   AVERAGE

You have all the characteristics necessary to feel like a fully empowered employee. At times you feel as though you have everything you need to be a truly effective employee, and at other times you feel as though you have no control over the things that happen on the job.

Continue to work at making decisions. Show your boss that you are competent and that you desire to have more control over your working environment.

59 to 70   HIGH

Yes, you are an empowered employee. You have more of an empowered feeling about your work than do 90% of your fellow employees. Your attitude is what makes your company successful. You have the necessary authority to make a difference and to influence others.

Keep up the good work, it is employees like you that make a difference.

the mean and the region labeled as HIGH consists of scores that are one standard deviation or more above the mean.

To use this scoring key (Figure 3), simply calculate a score, find the range it falls into on the key and read the corresponding interpretation. For example, let's consider a score of 15. Looking at the key, it is apparent that the empowerment level for an employee with a score of 15 is very low. An employee in this empowerment range feels a lack of authority on the job, little or no ability to influence the situations surrounding their job, like they cannot make a difference in their organization and that they lack the necessary resources to do their job. An employee with a low feeling of empowerment needs help. If the employee continues to work with a low level of empowerment, work will be both unfulfilling for the employee and for the organization.

Using the scoring key, it is possible to look at an individual's, department's or entire organization's empowerment level. However, when looking at the score for a department or overall organization, the median value should be used for interpretation instead of the arithmetic mean. The median value is the score at which half of the employees are above and half are below. From a managerial standpoint, the median value will provide the most meaningful assessment of a department's or organization's employee empowerment levels.

Expanding the Survey

When you have become comfortable with the idea of the empowerment survey and the employee survey process, you may want to consider expanding the survey. As was mentioned earlier, the employee survey provides a formalized communication link between employees and management. To help you maximize this line of communication, the employee survey can be expanded to cover more areas. In addition to determining empowerment levels, the employee survey can be used to evaluate job satisfaction, employee/management relations, benefits, pay, etc. When used properly, the employee survey is a very valuable information-gathering tool.

Developing an expanded employee survey also provides you with an excellent opportunity to initiate the empowerment process. At the St. Louis Bi-Chapter of the American Red Cross, an employee survey was developed which included the concerns of both managers and front line employees. While many companies claim to have a well-rounded employee survey, the St. Louis Red Cross actually developed one. Using a committee of employees from all levels of the organization, an employee survey was constructed containing the concerns of the entire organization. [2]

Including front line employees in the survey development process teaches managers to listen. In his book High-Involvement Management, Edward Lawler states, "Overall, it represents the beginning of the participative process since it allows some lower-level participants to affect the survey process." [3] In the give-and-take world of the survey development process, managers must learn to consider the suggestions of their subordinates. This simple but important lesson is one of the building blocks of a solid employee empowerment program.

Benchmarking (Monitoring Change)

One of the most talked-about terms in the area of measurement and quality improvement is benchmarking. Benchmarking is a self-improvement process by which a company develops measures of its performance and then compares the results of these measurements over time.

Benchmarks are used both internally and externally to monitor change and performance. Many companies have developed benchmarks to compare their performance with competitors and other businesses. Making comparisons with competitors and leading businesses allows a company to determine how well it is doing within its industry and the opportunity to identify and adopt the successful business practices of others. These types of benchmarks have been termed "strategic benchmarks." [4]

When working with employee empowerment, another type of benchmarking is essential. This type of benchmarking is referred to as "internal." Employee empowerment is ongoing process and requires careful monitoring to ensure its success. If your employees do not feel changes within themselves, or see changes taking place within your organization, it will be very difficult to keep them motivated. Internal benchmarks allow employees the ability to monitor their progress toward empowerment goals closely.

Establishing a Timetable

Benchmarking is a formalized process and requires a timetable for administration. Before you begin measuring empowerment levels, you should establish a formalized schedule so empowerment levels can be consistently tracked and evaluated over time.

As a rule of thumb, the frequency with which you measure an item is directly proportional to the importance of the item you are measuring and the speed with which the item you are measuring can actually show change. While employee empowerment levels may be important enough to measure on a day-to-day basis, they will probably not show any significant changes for a much longer period of time.

Therefore, for the first two years of your empowerment program, it is recommended that you measure empowerment levels on a quarterly basis. Figure 4 provides an example of the trends you might see over a four-month cycle. In this example it is apparent that the empowerment program is on track. Over the four-quarter cycle the trend for the three departments and the overall company is increasing.

After your empowerment program is moving along smoothly, it will be possible to offer measures on a less frequent basis. However, if you should ever notice a sharp decline in your trend, it is advisable to make the necessary adjustments in your empowerment program and begin taking measures on a more frequent basis. Once your program is back on track you can move back to less frequent measures.

Figure 4.

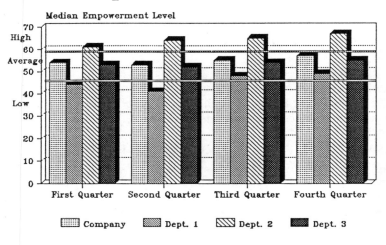

Empowerment Trends

Compare and Contrast Departments

The empowerment levels of the various departments in an organization can be calculated in much the same way they were for individuals. To insure that the empowerment score for a department is consistent with the average employee in the department, the median score should be used. (The median, or middle score, implies

that half of the employees have higher and half have lower scores.)
Once the median score is obtained for every department, comparisons
and analysis can be conducted.

Figure 5.

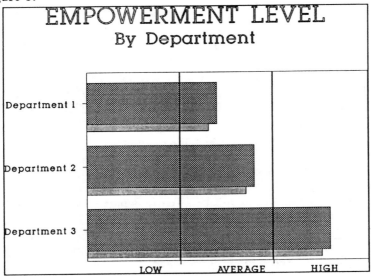

Departmental comparisons provide an excellent opportunity to
spot leading departments within your organization. In the example
presented in Figure 5, it is clear the average employee in Department
3 has a much greater feeling of empowerment than the average
employee in Department 1 or Department 2.

The information you obtain from this type of departmental
comparison may hold the key to empowering your entire organization.
A thorough analysis of the leading departments may reveal a set of
particular managerial practices, communication networks, training
programs, etc., that could be used to empower other departments in
your organization.

It is essential, however, that while looking for answers in your leading departments, you don't contaminate them with red tape and paper work. Altering the structure or requirements of a department may have an adverse or disempowering effect. And the last thing you want to do is harm your most empowered departments.

Be Careful of Competition

The employee empowerment process is not designed to encourage competition within your organization. Competition implies winners and losers, a dichotomy which is not part of the employee empowerment process. When conducted properly, all your employees will be winners with employee empowerment. The reward for an empowered employee is not in the form of money or plaques, rather, it is in the process itself. **(Monetary rewards and plaques may be part of an organization's reward and recognition program, but these rewards and awards shouldn't be given to departments or employees based on their feelings of empowerment.)**

Introducing competition into the employee empowerment process may result in resentment and distrust among managers and departments. The empowerment survey is designed to determine how empowered employees feel, and this is usually determined by things beyond the control of the employee. Therefore, employees cannot be blamed for a lack of training--if training is not provided to them, or for the inability to make decisions--if information is not made available to them, and so on. Pitting one department or employee against another based on their feelings of empowerment is not a fair or appropriate form of competition.

Pitting employees, departments, or teams against one another may also result in the loss of some of your company's most valued employees. When the executive teams used at Citicorp, Chemical Bank, General Electric, and CTE Corporation emphasized competition rather than cooperation, those ending up on the losing side typically left the company. [5]

Goal-Setting

Goal-setting is the final stage of the preliminary employee empowerment process. After setting employee empowerment goals, the process of empowering employees can begin.

The key to setting and achieving goals is the ability to dissect a situation into manageable tasks. The 1991 Touchstone Pictures release What About Bob? provides an excellent example of the goal-setting process.

Scene from What About Bob?

The scene takes place in the office of Dr. Leo Marvin (played by Richard Dreyfuss). Dr. Marvin has just indicated to his newly acquired psychiatric patient Bob Wiley (played by Bill Murray) that he can help Bob with his problems. The first step in Bob's treatment process is to read Dr. Marvin's newly published book, Baby Steps.

R. Dreyfuss: There is a ground-breaking new book that has just come out--now, not everything in this new book, of course, applies to you, but I'm sure you can see when you see the title exactly how it will help.

B. Murray: Baby Steps?

R. Dreyfuss: It means setting small reasonable goals for yourself, one day at a time, one tiny step at a time.

B. Murray: Baby Steps?

R. Dreyfuss: For instance, when you leave this office, don't think about everything you have to do to get out of the building. Just think of what you must do to get out of this room, and when you get to the hall--deal with that hall, and so forth.

B. Murray: Baby Steps.

For Bob, every activity and action in his life was a struggle. Even common tasks were difficult for him to complete. The only solution to his problem, was to break these tasks down into smaller and smaller parts, until he arrived at a part small enough he could complete. In this example, Bob's overall goal was to get home. However, to accomplish this overall goal, several much more manageable goals were set. Each one getting him closer to his apartment door.

While the scene from <u>What About Bob?</u> is somewhat humorous, the principle underlining this scene should be kept in mind when setting goals within your organization. Goals must be meaningful and realistic. When you establish goals that are impossible to achieve, you are setting yourself up for failure. Failing to achieve a goal is not inherently bad, but failing to achieve goals set for a new program like employee empowerment could threaten the future of the entire program.

Goals should also be specific. If a goal is established to increase employee empowerment levels, your empowerment programs should target the areas covered on the employee empowerment survey. Focusing on items or areas not covered on the employee empowerment survey may not have a immediate or direct impact on employee empowerment levels.

You should also establish a timetable for measurement. A systematic timetable should be included with each goal to ensure things are on track. As with benchmarking, a preestablished timetable will demonstrate your commitment and intentions to continue on with the employee empowerment process.

Involve as many people in the goal-setting process as possible. Goal-setting is a good way to get people working together and the teamwork phenomenon will help with the overall empowerment process.

Developing an Employee Empowerment Action Plan

An employee empowerment action plan provides an organizational emancipator with the focus and direction needed to implement successful employee empowerment programs. The final section of this chapter is designed to help the organizational emancipator with the construction of an employee empowerment action plan.

An action plan is the next tangible sign an organization is interested in empowering its employees. Writing employee empowerment action plans provide evidence of commitment. It can take a tremendous amount of time and energy to construct a satisfactory action plan. Therefore, when an organization commits to the process of writing an action plan it is taking another important step toward empowering its employees.

The steps involved in developing an action plan are by no means chiseled in stone. While it is important to take a disciplined approach to the preparation of an action plan, it is essential to be flexible and allow for changes as the plan unfolds. It is rarely possible to have perfect foresight; when the unexpected does occur, the success of the action plan may hinge on proper adjustment.

Define an Objective

The first step in writing an employee empowerment action plan is to define an objective. The objective is the desired outcome of the action plan. In many cases, your objective may be the same as your goal, but in any case the objective must be clear and understandable. If an organization is going to strive to achieve an objective, it is critical that everyone work toward the same thing.

An objective should be written in such a way that it makes a difference when it is achieved. There is little reason to commit to achieving an objective if it will account for no differences in an organization when it is achieved.

To be successful, the objective must have the support and commitment of management. Without managerial support, it will be very difficult to get the financing, time and personnel required to achieve the objective.

Finally, the outcome of the objective must be desired by front line employees. If employees do not see the benefit of working toward an objective, it will be very difficult to encourage them to commit to the action plan. The best way to determine the attitudes of employees is to ask their opinions. Involving front line employees in the action plan development process will help to ensure their participation when programs are finally implemented.

Implement Strategy

Once the objective or goal is defined, the second step is to define and implement a strategy to achieve the objective. A strategy must be defined in such a way that it is appropriate to the objective. Also, you must be sure the strategy you define logically leads to your desired objective.

The strategy must also be easy to understand and implement. A vague strategy may result in several interpretations and multiple approaches to achieving the objective. When an organization fails to get everyone focused and committed to the same strategy, it loses the benefits of the team approach. Many times the team approach is necessary to ensure the success of the objective.

In addition, strategies which are difficult to administer are very unlikely to be implemented. It is human nature to put off difficult tasks, while completing easier ones first. When designing a strategy, you should keep this in mind. This is not to say, however, that all strategies will be easy to implement. Rather, when a strategy is designed, it is important to take special care to ensure all possible options and simplifications are considered.

Measurement and Evaluation

The final steps in the development of an action plan are measurement and evaluation. Measurement is a necessary step in determining the status of the objective. Monitoring the progress toward an objective will help to ensure the intentions of the action plan are being achieved.

Including an evaluation step allows you to review the strengths and weaknesses of your action plan. With the results of the evaluation, you can fine-tune your strategy, helping to improve your chances of achieving your objective.

Outline and Example

Figure 6 provides an example of the structure for an action plan designed to improve employee empowerment levels. Figure 7 provides an example of an action plan designed to increase empowerment levels through an enhanced communication program with employees.

Figure 6.

Action Plan to Improve
Employee Empowerment Levels

Check List

Step 1.   **Define Objective**

    A.   Statement of what is to be achieved.

    _____

    _____

    B.   Will the objective make a difference when it is achieved? ___Yes ___No

    (If Yes) What difference will it make?

    C.   Is there commitment by management to follow through with the objective? ___Yes ___No

    (If Yes) What is evidence of this commitment?

    D.   Does the objective focus on something desired by the employees? ___Yes ___No

    (If Yes) How do you know it is desired?

Figure 6, Cont.

Step 2.   Implement Strategy

A.   Statement of strategy.

_____

_____

B.   Is the strategy appropriate to the objective? ___Yes ___No

C.   Is the strategy easy to understand? ___Yes ___No

        (If Yes) Have you asked those responsible for implementing the strategy
        if it is easy to understand? ___Yes ___No

D.   Is the strategy easy to implement? ___Yes ___No

Step 3.   Measurement and Evaluation

A.   Has the objective been achieved? ___Yes ___No

        (If No) What is being done to assure that the objective is achieved?

        _____

        _____

B.   What are (were) the strengths and weaknesses of the strategy?

        Strengths   Weaknesses

        _____   _____

        _____   _____

        _____   _____

        _____   _____

C.   Have department supervisors committed to the program? ___Yes ___No

D.   Have you obtained measurable improvements in employee
        empowerment levels? ___Yes ___No

Figure 7.

Example

Check List

Step 1.   **Define Objective**

A.   Statement of what is to be achieved.

To increase employee empowerment levels through an enhanced

communication program with employees.

B.   Will the objective make a difference when it is achieved? _X_ Yes ___No

(If Yes) What difference will it make?

Employees will have a clearer understanding of the day to day

operations of the organization.

C.   Is there commitment by management to follow through with the objective? _X_ Yes ___No

(If Yes) What is evidence of this commitment?

A formal plan which has been approved by the organization's

board of directors.

D.   Does the objective focus on something desired by the employees? _X_ Yes ___No

(If Yes) How do you know it is desired?

Through an employee attitude survey.

Figure 7, Cont.

Step 2.   **Implement Strategy**

A.   Statement of strategy.

An employee newsletter which highlights both current and upcoming organizational activities will be published on a weekly basis. This newsletter will be distributed personally to all employees by departmental supervisors.

B.   Is the strategy appropriate to the objective? _X_ Yes ___ No

C.   Is the strategy easy to understand? _X_ Yes ___ No

(If Yes) Have you asked those responsible for implementing the strategy if it is easy to understand? _X_ Yes ___ No

D.   Is the strategy easy to implement? _X_ Yes ___ No

Step 3.   **Measurement and Evaluation**

A.   Has the objective been achieved? ___ Yes _X_ No

(If No) What is being done to assure that the objective is achieved?

Employees are being surveyed as to their readership of the newsletter.

B.   What are (were) the strengths and weaknesses of the strategy?

Strengths	*Weaknesses*
Employees can take the information with them.	*It is only one source of information.*
Promotes discussion among employees.	*Some employees don't like to read.*
Thorough and timely.	*Some supervisors just leave the newsletter in a stack for employees to pick up.*

C.   Have department supervisors committed to the program? _X_ Yes ___ No

D.   Have you obtained measurable improvements in employee empowerment levels? _X_ Yes ___ No

Chapter 3 Organizational Emancipation Breaking the Chains

"The history of mankind has been marked by struggle between those who govern and those who are governed. In each major conflict, regardless of time, place, and circumstance, the voice of rebellion against authority has manifested itself in the cry for freedom, liberty, human rights and human dignity. The underlying motivation is the desire for the right to participate in the decisions that affect one's welfare."

Irving Bluestone
Worker Participation in Decision Making [1]

The Emancipation Proclamation

Over 100 years ago, Abraham Lincoln issued the proclamation emancipating the slaves. While this was an unpopular decision with many government officials, Lincoln new freeing of the was the right thing to do. The Emancipation Proclamation provided Lincoln with a chance to satisfy the radical abolitionists in the North and to add a much needed moral cause to the Civil War.

In a somewhat parallel situation, American business is being forced to change the way it handles employees. The days of the autocratic leader and subservient employee are no longer always appropriate. International competition has eroded domestic market share and pushed many companies into the red. To combat this onslaught from abroad, business is beginning to realize it must utilize all of its available resources, including the creative abilities of its employees.

Organizational Emancipator

This new class of managers in charge of liberating organizations can be referred to as "**Organizational Emancipators.**" They untie the hands and remove the blindfolds of their employees. These managers no longer make their employees walk the plank. Instead, they allow the employees to participate in an exciting and viable organization.

"Empowering employees takes them off of the plank. It unties their hands and removes their blindfolds."

Organizational emancipators understand that effectiveness is limited when supervisors must continually answer and solve employee problems. They have found organizational performance to be enhanced when employees are allowed to handle the situations surrounding their jobs.

Capturing the EMPOWERED SPIRIT

Congratulations go out to all the organizations using empowered employees as one of their strengths. However, for those organizations without this strength, don't be disheartened; the feeling of employee empowerment can be captured.

Finding it in Yourself

It is nice to note that the potential to feel empowered is in all of us. It is not necessary to travel to distant lands or uncover thousands of stones looking for it. The empowered feeling exists in all of us; waiting to be realized.

"Employee empowerment will not be found hiding under a rock."

The first step in becoming an organizational emancipator is learning to manage yourself. Self-management involves "knowing one's skills and developing them effectively." [2] Only after developing an understanding of yourself will it be possible to fully understand and empower others. Self-administering the measurement tool discussed in Chapter 2 is an excellent way to evaluate your current empowerment level. Understanding your own level of empowerment is an important step in understanding how it affects others.

Second, as an organizational emancipator you must work to develop anticipatory skills. "Anticipatory skills entail projecting consequences, risks and trade-offs (having foresight); actively seeking to be informed and to inform (scanning/communicating); and proactively establishing working relationships (building trust and influence)."[3] Each of these skills will be necessary if an organizational emancipator hopes to successfully empower employees.

The Relinquishment of Power

"Two hours ago I could have said five words and been quoted in every capital of the world. Now I could talk for two hours and nobody would give a damn."

President Harry Truman, shortly after leaving office.

Our society places a tremendous value on power and being powerful. In fact, researchers have even described power as an addiction, with effects similar to those caused by drugs. "Power shows remarkable similarities in the course taken by those who are addicted. We also notice a high and, in case of its loss, painful withdrawal symptoms." [4]

When becoming an organizational emancipator it is essential to understand the difficulties with relinquishing power--both within yourself and with those around you. Letting go of power and losing its associated high will be unattractive. [5]

Power provides its users with many rewards. Therefore, as you begin the empowerment process it will be important to develop a new system of rewards: Rewards based on the sharing of power instead of its accumulation.

Confronting and moving past the authoritarian corporate culture that has rewarded employees all of their lives will not be an easy task. In fact, for some organizations it may take an entirely new generation of employees, a generation with new values, and a new outlook on the corporate structure.

Getting the Necessary Resources

The next step in the empowerment process is obtaining the necessary resources. As is discussed in Myth 3, an employee empowerment program does not always imply giving employees more power. Many times, organizations must provide newly freed employees with resources required to do their job efficiently and effectively.

These resources consist of (1) training, (2) education, (3) equipment, (4) facilities, and (5) time. Each resource must be provided in proper proportion to ensure success. (The empowerment tool discussed in Chapter 2 will help determine the proper levels of these resources.) To be able to provide these resources a company must commit capital. The empowerment process is not free and must have financing if it is to be successful.

Leading by Example

Leading by example is one of the most powerful things an organizational emancipator can do. Demonstrating the benefits of the empowerment process through personal testimony allows employees to see the benefits of the process first hand.

As a organizational emancipator you must live up to the values you claim to hold. [6] If the empowerment process is not legitimately embraced by the emancipator, employees will become skeptical and question the true benefit of committing to the process.

As an organizational emancipator, you must hold on to your values and become reliable and consistent. "A recent study showed people would much rather follow individuals they can count on, even when they disagree with their viewpoints, than people they agree with but who shift positions frequently." [7]

Communication

60% of the misunderstandings in business are due to poor listening.

80% of all business communications must be repeated.

Rarely is more than 20% of what top management says understood four levels below.

--University of Minnesota Study [8]

The establishment of effective organizational communication networks is a primary component of any successful employee involvement or empowerment program. A good communication system must be three-directional. Management must be able to communicate with employees, employees with management, and departments with other departments (see Figure 1).

Figure 1.

Three Directional Communication

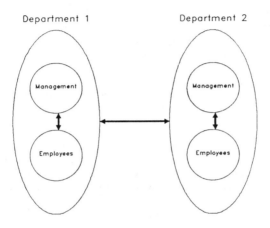

Department 1   Department 2

Management   Management

Employees   Employees

Communication can be obtained by several methods.   The following is a short list of some common methods of organizational communication:

1.   Newsletters
2.   Meetings
3.   Suggestion boxes
4.   Cross-departmental training
5.   The development of listening skills

No matter which methods are used in an organization, it essential to test their effectiveness.   Ask employees if they are finding out about the things they need to know.   And if they're not, modify the communication system so they do.

The same goes for communication from employees to management and communication between departments. If information is not being communicated, find out why and fix it.

Risk Taking

> *"We don't shoot people who make mistakes around here, we shoot people who don't take risks."*
>
> **Dick Liebhaber**
> **Director of Operations, MCI** [9]

As an organizational emancipator, you must find the courage to take risks and provide the freedom for others to take risks. At Prudential Insurance "before empowerment was possible, management had to be convinced that it was "safe" to relinquish power and delegate authority." [10]

The innovation and decision making necessary for an organization to excel into today's competitive marketplace will not be achieved until employees are allowed and convinced they can take risks. However, as Myth 7 outlines later in this book, the process of delegating authority and increasing responsibility should not be completed with haste. Many employees will need time to adjust to the new responsibilities associated with an empowered organization.

Leadership Styles

> *"The factor that empowers the work force and ultimately determines which organizations succeed or fail is the leadership of those organizations."* [11]

Managers have the option of using several different leadership styles. Each style has benefits and drawbacks. Understanding the needs and ambitions of employees allows for the selection of a leadership style to optimize employee empowerment levels. In many cases a manager may have to use different leadership styles for different employees and work groups.

Authoritarian

The authoritarian style of management is considered by many to be the traditional style of management. Based on the writings of Frederick W. Taylor, all decision making authority for an organization is to be positioned at the top and those at the organization's lower levels are responsible for doing.

For many businesses the authoritarian form of management is still widely practiced and in some cases it is justified (see Myth 4). However, many organizations have found much more efficient methods of managing employees through the use of more participative styles.

Mentoring

Mentoring is a style of leadership similar to an apprenticeship. While mentors do not maintain strict authoritarian control over employees, they are still the primary decision makers.

Mentors work to make employees self-directed and skilled employees. However, under a mentor, employees are not encouraged to be innovative or find new methods of doing their job.

Mentoring has been found to be very effective in occupations requiring a specific skill or in the development of a trade. In the long run, an employee who has been managed by a mentor should be able to complete all aspects of a job without asking questions or permission.

Coaching

The use of the term coach to describe a business leader is a relatively new. "A coach is someone who has an ongoing, committed partnership with a player/performer and who empowers that person or team, to exceed prior levels of play/performance." [12] Coaches are less likely to pass judgment on the performance of an employee, and instead provide constructive feedback.

It is important to note coaching is still not a completely participative form of management. While it does focus on bringing out the individual talents of the employees, it still is not a leadership style designed to make employees leaders of themselves. Coaching implies the need for a leader who directs the activities of employees.

Coaching is a very effective leadership style for motivating employees and improving organizational efficiency and output.

LEADERSHIP STYLES

Participative Coaching Mentoring

Free Rein◄ ████████▒▒▒▒▒▒▒▒ ►Autocratic

↑↑↑↑↑↑↑↑↑↑
Work teams

Employee Empowerment Can Take Place at Any
Place Along this Continuum

Participatory Management

Participatory management consists of allowing employees the opportunity to provide input into the decisions made in an organization. The degree to which management actually listens to what employees say determines where this type of leadership falls on the free rein--authoritarian continuum.

Participatory management is an excellent way to improve organizational efficiency, provided employees are properly trained and willing to participate. However, as Myth 11 points out later in this book, an employee empowerment program does not have to achieve a full degree of participatory management to be successful.

Work Teams

Work teams can fall anywhere on the free rein--authoritarian continuum. The level of commitment management must allow a team in order to function autonomously determines where on the continuum they fall. However, because of their nature, most teams falls somewhere around the participative region of the continuum.

Work teams have demonstrated a tremendous ability to improve specific organizational functions. Many times the effectiveness of a team is dependent on the equal participation of all team members.

Free Rein

Free rein is a leadership style which focuses on staying completely out of the way of employees. Under a free rein form of leadership, employees are allowed to do whatever they think is necessary to be successful. This type of leadership is not appropriate for most organizations, but it is used to some extent with certain types of professionals (Lawyers, doctors, consultants, etc.).

*"Organizational emancipators become committed to
the process of freeing employees."*

No matter what leadership style is chosen, usually there will be opportunities for improving empowerment levels. The organizational emancipator must strive to make others leaders of themselves. If an employee must have someone to rally around, or tell them what to do, they will continue to be subordinate and organizational effectiveness will suffer.

Establishing Commitment

Establishing commitment is essential to ensuring that a lasting emancipation permeates an organization. To obtain commitment, the emancipator must build trust, motivate and place confidence in employees. At PG&E they were quick to realize that without a strong concerted effort, they would never build the momentum required to make real improvements. [13]

A major component in establishing the commitment of employees, is demonstrating the commitment of the organization. Demonstrating organizational commitment can be done in many ways, but one of the best involves specifying the importance of employees and their empowerment in the corporate mission statement.

An organization's mission statement contains the primary reasons an organization exists and the values it deems important. The organizational mission is the foundation for all organizational planning and direction (see Figure 2). Therefore, including the importance of employees in the mission statement demonstrates the commitment of an organization to the empowerment process.

Figure 2.

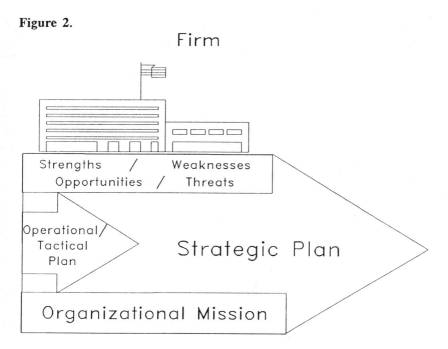

Firm

Strengths / Weaknesses
Opportunities / Threats

Operational/
Tactical
Plan

Strategic Plan

Organizational Mission

Once an organization has developed a mission statement including the importance of employees and employee empowerment, it will then be possible to conduct a new strategic planning process using the development and retention of employees as an organizational strength.

Strategic Plan

Alice in Wonderland
Conversation with Cheshire Cat

Alice: Would you tell me, please, which way I ought to go from here?

Cat: That depends a good deal on where you want to get to.

Alice: I don't much care where--

Cat: Then it doesn't matter which way you go.

With a newly crafted mission, an organization needs to develop a plan for the future. Without a plan it will be difficult for employees to understand an organization's future direction; therefore, it will be difficult for an empowerment program to take shape.

A strategic plan must take into consideration the entire environment an organization operates in. There are several books that discuss the entire strategic planning process, so for the sake of keeping things focused, we will only discuss the strategic issues relating to employees and employee empowerment.

As has been discussed throughout this book, employees should be viewed as an organizational strength. Therefore, when conducting your SWOT (Strengths, Weaknesses, Opportunities, Threats) Analysis, it is important to list employees as a strength. (However, if employees are an organizational weakness, a strategy must be developed to convert them to a strength.) The strategic plan should address specific ways the organization can increase the retention of employees and improve their loyalty.

Employees also provide an organization with a tremendous opportunity. Given that many employees are working far below their potential (see Introduction), investing in training and education provides the organization with an excellent chance to improve long-term performance.

Developing a strategy of increased worker participation and empowerment may also lead to innovation and improved efficiency. In the long run, to be successful organizations must be able to improve efficiency and develop new products. The competition will never be far behind, and so it is essential to maximize the abilities of employees. Include them in your mission statement, your strategic plan, in your day-to-day operational plans, and list them as an organizational strength.

Breaking down the corporate power structures that have endured for generations will not be an easy task. However, just as Abraham Lincoln used the Emancipation Proclamation during the Civil War, many organizations are realizing that employee emancipation may be the last hope for their survival.

How much change is necessary?

At Xerox, David Kearn said, "Most of us
who are running major companies may not
yet understand how much we will have to
(do) differently to be successful." [14]

Part II Myths and Realities

The analysis of hundreds of completed employee empowerment surveys has revealed several interesting facts about the concept. This section of the book is written to point out and clarify many of the generalized preconceived myths about employee empowerment.

We often talk of rules without their exceptions. With employees this cannot be done. Employees are a group in which, in many cases, the exceptions are as important as the rules. Employees are unique individuals, each with differing needs and personalities. Understanding the full reality of employee empowerment is essential as an organization strives for perfection.

Myth 1: Employee empowerment lessens the role of management.

Reality

Believe it or not, not all mangers are open and accepting of the idea of employee empowerment. Many fear that by empowering employees, their organizational role will somehow be diminished. They are afraid they are going to lose something they worked hard to acquire.

"I'll have nothing to do with employee empowerment if it means I will loose responsibility."

Uncovering these fears is not an easy task. Like most of us, managers are hesitant to reveal their insecurities. In fact, they have dreamed up numerous reasons why employee empowerment should not, or can not, be adopted in their organization. One manager even went so far as to say, "Employee empowerment is really part of a master plot designed by front line employees to take over America's corporations." Laugh if you wish, but this is the type of excuse that would make the John Birch Society proud.

Empowering employees may require managers to loosen up their reins. But this still doesn't mean their roles will be lessened.

Employee empowerment should focus on allowing people to do the jobs they were hired to do. If this means managers have to back off, so be it. Employees have a right to be able to learn and grow with their jobs.

Managers of empowered employees will not have their role lessened. Their roles may change, but they definitely will remain important. (The exception to this rule is for those who work in purposeless positions in top-heavy organizations. These employees should be on the lookout for anything that threatens the status quo.)

As an "Organizational Emancipator," the managerial role becomes one of coach and leader. Newly empowered employees require guidance and someone in a position to rally around. In this new role, managers will not be making the decisions for their employees; rather, they will provide the structure and framework from which the employees themselves can make good decisions.

Providing Resources

As managers encourage the empowerment process, they must make sure employees have the necessary resources to do their jobs. If there are reasons why the resource needs of employees cannot be filled then they must be told. Otherwise it may be necessary to realign their expectations.

While it is necessary in some cases, realigning employee expectations should be a last resort method in the employee empowerment process. The realigning of expectations involves effectively communicating to employees, what is, and what is not possible for the organization. However, before a manager rejects employee resource requests, an honest effort should be made to fulfill them. Employees can tell when their managers are lying.

Making a difference

Another role as organizational emancipator is to let employees know they make a difference. The organizational emancipator should explain to each employee how he or she fits into the overall picture of the organization. The "cog-in-the-wheel" analogy has no place in the empowering process. Employees need to know more. Employees need to feel they are doing something worthwhile.

The job of the organizational emancipator is much like that of a football coach. Although not all positions on a football team receive equal glory and recognition, it is the job of the coach to make each player understand the importance of his position. (Writing from the standpoint of a former offensive tackle, experience has revealed that a good coach can make all the difference in the world.)

As a coach explains the role of every player in a play, so must the organizational emancipator explain the role of every employee at work. A good organizational emancipator will pat employees on the back and congratulate them when they do a good job.

Increasing authority

In some cases, it may be necessary to provide employees with more authority. Allowing employees to make more of their own decisions will take some of the load off managers. Even if authority is granted for the sake of efficiency and has nothing to do with empowerment, it makes good sense. Employees hold a position in an organization for a reason; it is important they have the authority to do their job.

The role of the organizational emancipator is to guide employees in their use of authority. Organizational emancipators do not make the decisions for employees; instead, they are there to ensure employees are headed in the right direction.

Input and Suggestions

Organizational emancipators must also encourage employee input and suggestions. Because, employees experience problems firsthand, they should have input into how they are solved.

In addition, employees need to know that their input counts and that they can influence the decisions effecting their job. It is not enough to solicit input and suggestions from employees if nothing is done with the information. In fact, failure to follow-up on employee suggestions may actually lower employee empowerment levels. The organizational emancipator must let employees know their needs will not only be listened to, but their suggestions and input will be followed up and acted upon.

It's not easy

Nobody said the employee empowerment process would be easy. In fact, for a manager, it may be one of the more difficult tasks ever attempted. Understanding how the role of a manager changes with an employee empowerment program is essential to making it work. However, managers should not be worried an employee empowerment program will lessen their roles.

Final note

There are situations in which the role of the manager will not change at all. As other myths in this book reveal, some employees already feel fully empowered, and others may have no interest in the empowerment process. So, before a manager takes any major steps toward becoming an Organizational Emancipator, it is essential to find out whether there is a need. Using the measurement tool developed in Chapter 2, it is possible to determine the empowerment levels of employees as well as the need for employee empowerment programs.

Myth 2: Supervisors or managers will always feel more empowered than their employees.

Reality:

During the development of the employee empowerment measurement tool, an amazing discovery was made. While testing a final draft of the survey instrument with the other employees in my office, I was surprised to find that my secretary felt a higher level of empowerment than me. At first I was shocked; I had been under the impression supervisors would always feel more empowered than their employees. So, to determine if this truly was the case (or if I was a single exception), I decided to look at this relationship in other organizations.

While these subsequent studies did reveal a relationship between an individual's position and his of her feeling of empowerment, it did not ensure it. Some employees just feel more empowered than their supervisors.

This finding, or realization, serves to stress two important issues- -the importance of measuring employee empowerment levels and developing empowerment programs for all levels of an organization.

Measurement first

As was discussed in Chapter 2, the measurement of employee empowerment levels should be conducted prior to the development of any employee empowerment enhancement programs. Measuring empowerment levels will allow a manager to locate the areas within an organization in need of the employee empowerment process. In addition, measurement can also help in determining the content that these programs should focus on.

Without measurement, it is next to impossible to pinpoint the specific areas in need of help. Employee empowerment is a feeling. Different employees may have different levels of this feeling. Enhancing the feeling of empowerment involves increasing the abilities of employees to be both proactive and reactive to the situations surrounding their jobs.   Concentrating on the areas necessary to improve these proactive and reactive abilities will insure that employee empowerment dollars are spent as cost effectively as possible.

Empowerment at all levels

The second important issue is to develop employee empowerment programs for all levels of an organization.   Because there are managers as well as employees in need of the empowerment process (measurement will reveal this), it is important that specific programs be developed for each group. It may even be necessary to develop programs for classifications smaller than the manager and front line employee groups.

Specialized employee empowerment programs will guarantee maximum benefits are received. As is discussed with Myth 4, a universal empowerment program for all employees is not the answer.

The empowering process involves matching the capabilities, desires and ambitions of an employee with his or her position. This process may be easy with front line employees, but can be very difficult with those at the management level.

As employees climb the corporate ladder, office politics and factors external to the organization begin to play much stronger roles. The items affecting a middle manager's decision making process can be complex.   Understanding this is a critical part of any viable employee empowerment program.

The organizational emancipator must not only be concerned with subordinates, but also with peers and supervisors. In light of this, one element necessary in many empowerment programs (particularly those designed for management) is expectation modification.

Expectation Modification

The level of empowerment an employee feels is relative. From employee to employee, feelings of empowerment vary. It is not uncommon for employees who hold the same title and work for the same supervisor to have different feelings of empowerment.

It is also important to note that the empowerment feeling is effected by expectations. Feelings of empowerment are the result of the varying levels of expectations employees have as to what they can and should be able to do on the job. If an employee's expectations are in accordance with what is actually possible at their job, it will be much easier to empower them.

If it is not possible for an organization to change its working climate (i.e., giving employees the resources, training, the feeling that they count, the opportunity to be heard, etc.) then employees must be informed as to what they can expect. An organization's empowerment levels can vary from top to bottom. It is critical that all employees, including managers, have their empowerment levels checked. If there is any truth to the idea of leading by example, then empowerment at the management level is certainly as important as it is on the front lines.

Myth 3: Empowering employees always implies giving them more power.

Reality:

The empowering of employees can take place in many ways, some of which do not require giving the employee more power. As you will remember from Chapter 1, power is defined as the authority and ability implied by an employee's position in an organization. While increasing an employee's level of power may be one of the ways of increasing their empowerment level, it can be shown that the empowering process can take place without implying anything different about an employee's position.

Listening

The feeling of employee empowerment can be improved by managers who listen. Empowerment levels increase when employees are given the opportunity to be heard. However, all the benefits of listening are negated when an organization fails to respond to what employees say. When it is all put together, listening and being responsive to employee comments are excellent ways of empowering employees.

Training

*"We can't support a customer oriented objective
without having a strong emphasis on training."* [1]

Larry McMahan
Vice President Human Resource Development
Federal Express

The empowered feeling can be enhanced through training. Employees who lacks the necessary training to do their jobs may feel as though they are unable to solve some of the problems resulting from their jobs. Managers should be on the lookout for employees who could benefit from additional training. Training programs can give employees the extra edge needed to be successful in their jobs.

It is important to note that the need for training may not be as obvious as one might think. To be successful, employees may need training in areas which seem to have no relation to their job. At Disney even the street sweepers are given four days of training. "Disney wants sweepers who are able to answer guests' questions about the park." [2]

Encouraging advanced education by paying for college expenses is an excellent method of empowering employees. While this may seem to be an excessive expense, Carl's Jr. actually saved money by doing it. Over a two-year period, the fast food restaurant chain saved $145,128 dollars in turnover costs, while spending only $90,000 on tuition and education fees. [3]

*"Some employees may need assistance or training
if they are ever to feel empowered."*

Encouragement

Encouragement by management and fellow employees is another way of improving empowerment levels. The support of peers and supervisors will help to provide employees with the feeling things are being done right. Employees will need this backing if they are to ever feel empowered.

Necessary Resources

Employees must also be provided with the necessary resources to do their jobs. Employees will never develop feelings of empowerment if their equipment is constantly failing or if they cannot get the tools required for a job. An employee's ability to be proactive and reactive to the situations surrounding his or her job is directly dependent upon the resources available.

Information

*"If you can't say something simply,
you don't really understand it."*

Albert Einstein

It is also essential to keep employees informed. Lack of communication is one of the major causes for low employee empowerment levels. If employees need to know things so they can successfully do their job, it is essential that they be informed. Memos and bulletin boards may not be enough. To be effective employees may require one-to-one contact.

Jack Stack, manager of Springfield Remanufacturing, takes the process of information one step further. At this business, "every employee understands exactly how money is made or lost, and exactly how she or he influences the process of making it or losing it." [4] Because of this level of information, employees are able to take a much higher degree of ownership in their job--ownership which enhances the empowerment process.

Matching

Employees should be matched to their tasks in accordance with their training and experience. When assigning jobs, managers cannot play favorites. Employees must be allowed to do the jobs they were trained for. Based on job descriptions, employees have expectations about their jobs. Therefore, enhancing empowerment levels can be achieved by making sure an employee does the job he or she was hired for.

Decisions

Employees must be allowed to make more decisions regarding the events occurring in their jobs. Even if these decisions start small and gradually increase in importance, managers must be willing to let this process occur.

Increasing the decision making capabilities of employees actually serves to solve two problems. Not only will this process increase the empowerment level of employees*, it will also free up managers from the responsibility of making all decisions.   An employee empowerment process encouraging employees to make more decisions can be beneficial to an organization.

Several Ways

It has been shown there are several procedures for increasing the empowerment level of employees. The old myth--**empowerment can only be increased by increasing power,** is just that--a myth. Employee empowerment can be enhanced through several methods. However, finding the methods appropriate for any one organization or department will require measurement and analysis, a process taking time and commitment.

*   **There is a special case where this will not occur.
See Myth 4.**

Myth 4: A universal empowerment program will lead to an entire organization of highly empowered employees.

Reality:

Unfortunately, too many businesses believe this myth to be true and have adopted employee empowerment programs which may not be achieving their desired results. Simply put, the "cookie cutter" approach will not work with employee empowerment. For empowerment programs to be completely effective, employees must be treated as individuals.

Employee empowerment is a process that must focus on the exceptions as well as on the rules. In fact, in some organizations, there may be nearly as many exceptions as those that fit in with the rule. Managers must remember employees are individuals, and every effort must be made to treat them as such. Many coaches are successful because they understand the importance of understanding individuality. Rick Pitino, head coach of the University of Kentucky basketball team says, "You can motivate an entire team to perform on a certain night, but you have to understand what motivates every individual." [1]

Even if an organization consisted of a homogeneous group of employees, this still does not imply that the employees in one organization will be the same as employees in another. Therefore, employee empowerment programs can't simply be copied from one company to the next. Work must be done with each organization in setting up its own appropriate employee empowerment program. Employee empowerment programs must focus on enhancing the way employees feel about their work. It is important to keep in mind that programs and policies may affect two employees or organizations very differently.

In most cases, developing an universal employee empowerment program for all employees will ensure that either some employees fail or that others will get nothing out of the process. Because there are usually exceptions, (both higher and lower) to the rule, universal employee empowerment program will not be appropriate for every one.

Employees with low levels of empowerment

First, let's look at how a universal employee empowerment program could destine some employees to failure. Take, for example, an employee empowerment program designed to increase the decision making ability of employees. A program such as this may be quite appropriate for capable and competent employees. However, not all employees are capable and competent.

In fact, giving some employees more responsibility without first giving them additional training may be like throwing them to the sharks. Many employees lack the business and economic education necessary to make competent suggestions and decisions. [2] Therefore, instead of increasing empowerment levels, as the program was designed to do, it might actually decrease the feeling of empowerment with the less capable and competent employees.

*"Be sure employees have adequate training
before giving them more responsibility."*

"Failure to do this may be like feeding them to the sharks."

No Empowerment, Please

A second example is derived from the assumption that all employees want to be empowered. We have assumed up to this point all employees want to be empowered. While, this is generally the case, I have found some exceptions to this rule. One Northern Telecom employee said, "You're asking me to take on more responsibility, to make decisions I thought you were paid to make." [3]

In addition, many part-time employees have told me they are working solely for the money. These employees would just as soon have very little responsibility and few or no decisions to make. While this group may only make up a small portion of an organization's labor force, it is important to keep this element in mind. Managers cannot assume that all employees will be open and accepting to the employee empowerment process.

Off days

*"How would you like a job where,
if you make a mistake, a big red
light goes on and 18,000 people boo?"*

**Former hockey goalie
Jacques Plante**

An employee's desire for empowerment may also have some "off days." Managers must remember there will be days and times when normally competent and conscientious employees will not want to or will make the wrong decisions. Managers must understand these times will come and go with all employees. The manager's job is to be aware and guide employees when empowerment levels decide to take a "temporary leave." At Prudential Insurance, their "new culture offers a 'Safety Net' for those who try and fail, providing they correct their mistakes and try again." [4] Managers can rest easy in the fact, as the empowerment process progresses, these temporary lapses will usually occur farther and farther apart.

Immature or maturing employees

Managers should use caution with the empowerment process when dealing with immature or maturing employees. While these employees may have a strong desire to be empowered, it may be best to take them down the road of empowerment slowly. The management and development of empowerment programs for immature and maturing employees can be one of the biggest challenges faced by a manager.

Highly Empowered Employees

The development of an employee empowerment program for the least common denominator will have little or no effect on those employees with moderate to high levels of empowerment. In fact, if highly empowered employees are forced to sit through remedial training programs, it might actually lower their levels of empowerment.

Managers must be careful not to change the working environment for employees with the desired feelings of empowerment. Change, in this case, may actually alter the working conditions that have made these employees feel empowered in the first place.

Transient Employees

A special class of worker not mentioned earlier is the transient employee. The transient employee can be best described as an employee who works for an organization for a very short period of time (six months or less).

Mangers should be cautious when attempting to empower transient-type workers. Certainly the costs and benefits of training programs should be analyzed before they are initiated. Many times it is not worth the expense to train an employee who will stay with an organization only a short time.

While managers should be cautious in expending a lot of money empowering transient employees, they should also be careful they are not encouraging a transient way of life. Some employees may have a transient nature merely because they have not found a job in which they feel empowered. So, while managers may be justified in feeling cautious about spending larger sums of money of training transients, they should not encourage a transient nature by overlooking other methods to enhance the transient's feeling of empowerment.

Safe universal employee empowerment procedures

While it is true a universal employee empowerment program will not necessarily lead to highly empowered employees, there are a few procedures all organizations can feel safe in using. The first of these "safe" procedures is providing information. Keeping employees informed about the issues affecting their jobs is important no matter how empowered employees feel. The only caution in connection with providing information is not to inundate employees with memos and long esoteric meetings. When providing information, managers should keep their messages short and to the point. Also, before finishing, they should make sure employees understand the information provided. If the information is not phrased in language that is understandable to the employee, then the attempt at communication will fail. Managers must take special care to make sure employees not only receive information, but that they also understand what it means.

Another safe empowering procedure is encouragement. Again, no matter how empowered an employee feels, additional encouragement from a manager or supervisor cannot hurt. An employee needs to know when he of she is doing a good job. For some employees, encouragement is the fuel keeping them going. The nice thing about encouragement is it is easy to provide and it doesn't cost anything.

While I'm sure there are other safe employee empowerment procedures, the last one I will discuss is active listening. Employees deserve the right to be heard, no matter how empowered they are. Listening is not an easy task for some managers to master. However, responding to what employees say may be even harder. Managers must work to listen actively to employee requests and comments. Active listening is an effective employee empowering procedure no matter what the status of the employee.

Myth 5: Making an organization thinner will result in more highly empowered employees.

Reality:

Although it may be true that several layers in an organization may actually stifle the employee empowerment process, it is not necessarily true that thinning an organization results in a more highly empowered organization. A thinner organization does not imply a more empowered organization. If employees on the front line do not achieve competency or develop responsibility, even a two-level organization may have employee empowerment problems.

Yet, while a thinner organization does not imply a more empowered organization, it is true the employee empowerment process may allow an organization to become thinner. IBM made a major change in its organization in early 1988. This change involved the elimination of central staffs and the creation of broad product groups. "IBM's top management intended with this change to push decision making down the hierarchy and flatten the organization." [1]

When organizational thinning takes place, it implies the displacement of some employees and fewer opportunities for advancement for those who are left. If an organization mishandles the termination of a number of middle managers, it will lead to trouble. In fact, the termination of large numbers of employees can breed the types of feelings the employee empowerment process attempts to remove. Organizations should use special care when terminating employees no matter what the reason.

Organizational Spreading

One possible marriage between the employee empowerment process and organizational thinning is the idea of organizational spreading. Instead of terminating employees with a thinning process, employees can be used to expand and spread an organization. The spreading-out process will help to alleviate some of the problems created by terminating employees and may actually lead to new business development opportunities. The spreading of an organization allows for the removal of the layers of middle management without the termination of a large number of employees. Instead of employees being terminated, new positions are created, either through an expansion of services or through the development of new products.

While organizational spreading may be the answer to a lot of important questions, managers must also be aware this process can have problems of its own. Organizations should take care to ensure that the spreading process is carefully planned and implemented. Even though the spreading-out process will help to eliminate fear and unrest, many middle managers may view the process as a demotion. Therefore, it is essential for the process to be carried out in a positive manner. Managers must be brought to recognize that this process is best in the long run, and with it managers will have fewer levels of red tape and politics to contend with.

When it's unavoidable

While it is best to exhaust all other possibilities before thinning an organization, sometimes it can't be avoided. Tight budgets, plant shut-downs, the list goes on and on. However, if work force reduction must take place, it is essential for the organization to retain the trust of the remaining employees.

When asked about Bank of America's restructuring process that lasted from 1985 to 1988 and resulting in the loss of 34,000 employees, Executive Vice President Robert Beck had the following comment:

> "There's a natural tendency for the wagons to circle whenever there is a serious threat. We had to make sure that there was one big circle. The worst scenario is to have a lot of small circles shooting at each other. Infighting can be extremely unproductive, with people getting hit in the crossfire." [2]

Several questions must be answered if an organization hopes to maintain its integrity during the downsizing process. Matejka and Presutti [3] have come up with the following list of essential questions.

Downsizing Questions

1. What problem (opportunity) caused the personnel reduction and who was responsible?

2. Are the cuts truly necessary?

3. How are the cuts being made?

4. How much time, money, and care are being spent to help the laid-off employees deal with the trauma?

5. How well is all this being communicated?

6. Why should I believe that the future will be any different from the past?

7. What is the company doing to heal the wounds of the survivors?

The empowering process will be difficult if employees are constantly looking over their shoulders, wondering who is next. In situations like this, management must provide employees with information until they understand. Employees must be brought to understand the reasons for the terminations and layoffs. Philips Lighting Company's Vice President of Human Resources Kevin Doran says, "The thing you must keep emphasizing is that you are making changes because of market realities, not for arbitrary reasons." [4] The employee empowerment process can continue only after employees understand and their negative feelings have been left behind.

Retraining

To help alleviate many of the problems associated with downsizing, many organizations have developed retraining programs and outplacement services. Reebok retrains its former managers because "even in a recession there is no shortage of job opportunities for highly skilled people." [5] Retraining efforts and outplacement services provide evidence that a company cares. In fact, in many cases these procedures are as important to the employees leaving an organization as to those who stay. For employees who leave, these programs make finding a new job much easier; for those who stay, these programs reaffirm a relationship of trust.

Complex issue

The relationship between organizational thinning and employee empowerment is a complex issue. While organizational thinning may be an inevitable event for some organizations, if it is not done correctly it can have a devastating effect on empowerment levels. By maintaining an open line of communication and providing outplacement services and retraining programs for former employees, companies have been able to remove many of the negative aspects of downsizing.

Myth 6: **Empowering employees is a quick fix for an organization.**

Reality:

"All employees are hereby instructed to take more control over their work."

Just recently I was at a conference attended by individuals holding management level and human resource positions. While socializing with a small group of these conference-goers, I was surprised to find such an extensive interest in employee empowerment. Each of us was sharing our experiences, when one of the managers began to tell about his employee empowerment program.

"It took me two weeks to implement. We started one Monday morning and by the following Friday afternoon, we were finished. During this time we had an outside consultant come in for three days and give pep talks to all the employees and on the other days we worked on reevaluating our job descriptions. It was a lot of work, but we did it. I'm sure the employees feel better, because the management and staff certainly do."

Wouldn't it be wonderful if this was all it took. Two weeks and you're finished. However, the reality of an employee empowerment program is not a quick fix; rather, it is a long-term commitment. Managers would be wise to think of employee empowerment as a process and not a state. High levels of employee empowerment cannot be achieved and maintained with a one- or two-week program. Once initiated, the employee empowerment process becomes an ongoing part of an organization.

The process of empowering employees may even take a generation until it takes hold. In a recent article, one expert concluded that "General Motors may have to wait for the next generation of leaders to come out of the lower levels, where they have worked with joint efforts and seen its accomplishments, before the company can truly transform itself." [1]

"Empowering employees is more than blowing smoke."

Culture

To be successful, the employee empowerment process must become part of an organization's culture. The goal of an organization should be to increase the overall feeling of employee empowerment during every hour, minute and second of every day. To accomplish this, the employee empowerment enhancement process must be built into an organization's culture. Prudential Insurance initially found employees resisting their empowerment efforts. "They felt safer in the old culture where they had lower levels of responsibility and accountability." [2]

When looking at employee empowerment from a committed standpoint, it becomes clear it cannot be classified in the category of quick fixes. In fact, once it is initiated, the employee empowerment process will never end. Preparing employees for the present, as well as the future, is all part of the employee empowerment process. As an organization changes, employees must be prepared to change with it. At Quad/Graphics, Chief Harry Quadracci has said that for his organization, training will not be enough. "An orientation toward perpetual skill enhancement--the handmaiden of continuous improvement and continuous innovation--must become the norm." [3]

For some organizations, keeping employees up-to-date will be much more difficult than in others. If an organization exists in an environment of rapidly changing technology or competition, the empowerment process may require substantial ongoing training programs and communication channels.

If, however, an organization exists in a stable market, with little or no changes in technology and competition, the need for ongoing training programs may not be necessary. From organization to organization, it is important for managers to establish the needs of their employees. Once the needs are understood, successful empowerment programs can be developed.

Training

One part of the employee empowerment process which cannot be conducted quickly is training. As was stated earlier, it may be necessary to retrain employees before they will feel empowered. If employees need to be trained or retrained, the employee empowerment process may take months, and in some cases, years.

Depending on the type of business, changing technologies may have a dramatic impact on the level of empowerment employees feel. The computer is a good example of a technological change that has had an impact on all types of business. When computers were first introduced, the feeling of empowerment by some employees hit rock bottom. However, after extensive training programs, many of these employees learned to feel comfortable with computers. Today, ongoing training programs help keep employees abreast of the changes taking place with computer hardware and software. Ensuring that employees feel comfortable with the equipment and situations surrounding their jobs is essential to enhancing their feeling of empowerment.

Responsible

Many employee empowerment programs are also focused on making employees more responsible. However, it can be disastrous to delegate responsibility to employees who are not prepared. Responsibility is something which must be earned over time. Responsibility should be carefully handed out to those who are ready and deserving of it.

Prepare A Plan!

The mere nature of employee empowerment implies it may take a lot of time and fine tuning to be successful. To ensure goals are attained and the process stays on track, managers must prepare a plan.

When an organization decides to become committed to the employee empowerment process, a thorough plan should be designed. During the early stages a plan can be vague and sketchy; however, after an empowerment program is initiated, it should become much more concrete. Specific goals should be written and action plans developed (see Chapter 2). A employee empowerment plan is a necessary step when following through with the employee empowerment process.

Mangers shouldn't settle for a two-hour, two-day or even a two-week program. The employee empowerment process should be developed so that it continually enhances an organization.

Myth 7: Employee empowerment will lead to only good things for an organization.

Reality

Risk is involved with empowering employees. Contrary to what many have said, employee empowerment is not a sure thing. The employee empowerment process entails many unknowns. Managers must always be on the lookout for potential problems.

The employee empowerment process may affect two employees or organizations differently. Managers must realize this and be ready to alter their programs or adopt new programs as the employee empowerment process unfolds.

Only Human

Contrary to what many managers may think, employees are only human. Given this mortal nature, mistakes and accidents can be expected to happen.

When designed properly, the employee empowerment process focuses on increasing the ability employees have to be both proactive and reactive to the situations surrounding their job. While many good things can result from the employee empowerment process, it is essential that managers not only be prepared for the expected, but also the possibility of the unexpected.

Overconfidence

One of the biggest problems often resulting from the employee empowerment process, is employee overconfidence. A primary goal of employee empowerment is to increase the level of confidence employees have with their jobs. However, care must be taken not to instill too much confidence in employees. Overconfident employees are not the desired outcome of the employee empowerment process.

Overconfident employees can cause more harm than good. Rash and hasty decisions resulting from overconfidence can be devastating to an organization. While the employee empowerment process is designed to encourage employees to make more and better decisions, the contrary may result from overconfidence.

Managers must be on the lookout for overconfident employees. The "cocky" nature of an overconfident employee is usually not in the best interest of an organization's service quality. High quality customer service requires employees who are caring and responsive. It requires employees to listen, not employees acting like they have heard it all before. Recognizing and controlling employee overconfidence is essential to ensuring an effective employee empowerment program and providing high quality customer service.

Independence

Independence is promoted by the employee empowerment process through the enabling of employees to be better able to handle the situations surrounding their jobs. Independence evolves as an employee's dependence on others in an organization is decreased. The type of independence employees gain from the employee empowerment process usually impacts an organization positively. However, there are cases when it does not.

One such case is when the independence results in employees who do not function together as a team. One of the goals of the employee empowerment process is to create an organization functioning as a team. When employee independence gets carried away the results can be just the opposite.

Managers must be conscious of problems with employee independence and work to ensure that the team concept is not lost. The presence of "isolationist"-type employees (employees who do not interact with others) is a sure sign of the lack of the team concept. If this should occur, managers should work to refocus their programs to encourage more teamwork among employees.

Problems with independence can also result when employees use the empowerment process as a justification for not listening to or recognizing authority. One manager told me his employees loved the empowerment process because it meant they didn't have to listen to their supervisors. This may seem funny, but it happens. Some employees will look for any excuse to do as they please.

"Employee empowerment may not be like finding a shamrock."

Therefore, the organizational emancipator must keep a firm hand on the employee empowerment process. Employees cannot be allowed to have unguided control. When implementing a process encouraging employees to make more decisions, managers and employees must both remember who is in control. While the employee empowerment process may relieve managers from many of the decisions they have to make, it should not alleviate their authority. Managers must remain in control to provide guidance and to ensure that the employee empowerment process remains on track. Then, as the employee empowerment process progresses and employee become committed, managers will have fewer and fewer reasons to exercise their authority.

Mistakes will happen

"Even the most empowered employees will make mistakes."

Managers must also remember even the most well intentioned employees will make mistakes. Mistakes occur regardless of an employee's feeling of empowerment or level of competence. Mistakes are a result of the human element in all of us. Managers must work employees through their mistakes in a manner that does not endanger the empowerment process.

The majority of employees do not desire to make mistakes any more than a manager likes to see them. However, if a group of employees is prone to making more than their share of mistakes, managers should look to see if more training or better equipment is needed. If this is not the case, then it may be a sign the employees are in over their heads.

Controlling the risk

The employee empowerment process is not without risk. However, the risk can be controlled. Managers need to be aware that employee empowerment will not always be a bed of roses. Recognizing the potential for the possibility of negative occurrences is the first step in controlling the risk.

Once this possibility is realized, managers can develop contingency plans for action. These contingency plans must take the treatment of employees into consideration. Employees must be treated with dignity and respect, even when they are wrong.

The second step is effectively handling the occurrence of problems. Effectively handling any of the potential negatives resulting from the employee empowerment process is as important as recognizing their occurrence. Using a contingency plan, managers will be prepared to handle any problems or employee mistakes while maintaining the integrity of the empowerment process. Effectively handling any problems with employees will bring an organization one step closer to their empowerment goals.

Myth 8:   Empowering employees is free.

Reality

To be successful, employee empowerment requires commitment and investment. As with most of the worthwhile endeavors an organization can undertake, a cost is involved with employee empowerment. Although the amount of this cost definitely varies from organization to organization, every organization committing to the employee empowerment process will have costs.

Employee empowerment is not as simple as giving a speech or writing a policy. The employee empowerment process requires much more. To be successful the employee empowerment process may require multiple speeches and several policies to be rewritten. Managers may have to spend hours developing and implementing communication channels and training programs. Organizations may need to purchase new equipment or develop an employee reward and recognition program.

There is a cost to anything an organization does in an attempt to increase employee empowerment levels. Even if the cost is not in the form of a direct capital outlay, a time commitment is always required to initiate the employee empowerment process. And when there is a time commitment, there is a cost.

Saves money

Employee empowerment may actually save an organization money. One of the prime objectives of the employee empowerment process is to increase the level of responsibility employees have with their jobs. Increasing employee responsibility levels can lead to a more efficient organization. The improvements in efficiency may then result in monetary savings.

Enhancing an organization's internal communication channels is another way employee empowerment can lead to cost savings. When managers develop a two-way open line of communication with employees, it is amazing what can happen. Allowing employees to suggest and recommend more efficient ways to do their jobs can result in tremendous savings for an organization. Even if each suggestion or idea saves only a little, over time these savings will add up.

Organizations with employees working in hazardous positions can also save money with a good employee empowerment program. Encouraging employees to be more responsible and responsive can result in a safer organization. Reducing the number of lost-time accidents and insurance claims is a very responsible way of using employee empowerment to reduce an organization's costs.

The manufacturing industry can use employee empowerment to increase product quality and reduce cost. Each time a poor quality product is produced, an organization must pay to have it repaired or replaced. Empowering employees to be more responsible and conscientious about their work is an excellent way of reducing the percentage of factory defects and overall costs.

Make additional money

In much the same way employee empowerment saves an organization money, it can also help an organization make additional profits. The employee empowerment process is conducive to new business development and the enhancement of current products and services.

As the empowerment process leads to better trained employees, these employees will in turn help to ensure high quality service and products; the cornerstone of an organization's future profits. Building a reputation for a solid product or service is much easier with empowered employees. The establishment of a good reputation for a product or service is an excellent way to use the employee empowerment process to help ensure an organization's future profits.

The two-way communication channels developed out of the employee empowerment process are also very effective in promoting new business development. Encouraging employees to express new ideas is just another way to use the employee empowerment process to enhance an organization's profits.

It's the right thing to do

Even if an organization can find no financial justification for implementing an employee empowerment program, remember, it's the right thing to do. Employee empowerment shouldn't be a cost issue. Employee empowerment is about allowing employees the opportunity to maximize their potential, a right every human should have. Managers and accountants stuck on the idea of cost should put themselves in the place of the unempowered employee.

Myth 9:   Everyone in an organization must be empowered for things to get better.

Reality:

It only takes the empowerment of one individual for things in an organization to get better. Organizations should not become disheartened if there are not immediate results with their empowerment programs. Very few programs or policies are immediately adopted by everyone in an organization. Even programs and policies in everyone's best interest will take time to adopt and implement.

"It only takes one to get things started."

It may take quite a lot of time before any results are realized from an organization's employee empowerment program. One by one, however, employees can be brought along. It is the job of the Organizational Emancipator or the manager in charge of the employee empowerment process to ensure things keep moving.

The more the merrier

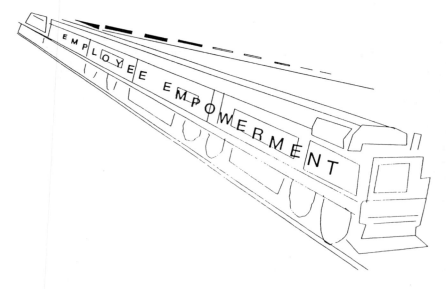

While it may only take one employee to get an empowerment program started, the process will gather speed like a locomotive as more employees commit to the process. Much of what is involved with the empowering of employees arises out of the relationships employees have with each other. As more employees commit to the underlying philosophy of empowerment, it will be much easier to increase the feeling of empowerment. But again, this is not an easy task. As good as employee empowerment may sound, getting people to commit to something, even something good for them, is not necessarily easy.

Managers must remember that some employees and supervisors have their own agendas. Care must be taken to ensure that the employee empowerment process is not exploited for individual advancement. As the employee empowerment locomotive begins to "chug," managers should bring along only those employees who are sincere about the process.

"I Don't Count"

Managers must also be aware of the employees who feel they just don't count. Deprogramming the "cog in the wheel" and the "my vote doesn't count" mentalities may require a significant effort. Employees need to brought to the understanding that everyone has a role and is important to an organization. If an organization desires to maximize the feeling of empowerment, it will require the participation of all employees.

Getting it going

The first step in the employee empowerment process is the commitment of one individual, the organizational emancipator. The organizational emancipator must understand employee empowerment levels will not rise overnight. Being the first to commit to the employee empowerment process, organizational emancipators must truly believe their organizations will be better off by increasing the feeling of empowerment among employees. Without this deep level of commitment, it will be difficult to gain the participation and support of the organization's other employees.

Coupled with the feeling of commitment is the need for focus. The organizational emancipator must have a clear plan for implementing the employee empowerment process. Employee empowerment levels may be low for various reasons. Therefore, making the changes necessary to increase employee empowerment levels will require a clear strategy.

Organizational emancipators can take heart in the fact that things will get easier with each additional employee committing to the employee empowerment process. There will always be setbacks and obstacles to moving the employee empowerment process forward, but a deep level of commitment and a clear focus will help to ensure the program's overall success.

Myth 10: Employees are not empowered and therefore need to be.

Reality

As was mentioned in Chapter 2, "Employee empowerment should be measured prior to planning or implementing any programs or policies...." Without measuring employee empowerment levels, it is difficult to know whether an employee empowerment program is needed. Although many managers and consultants automatically assume employee empowerment programs are necessary, in some cases they may be a waste of time, money, and in some cases they may even be counterproductive.

Waste of time and money

Employee empowerment requires the commitment of an organization's time and money. Therefore, before an organization jumps into the employee empowerment process, it is essential to ascertain whether there a need. Believe it or not, some employees already have very high levels of empowerment. When this is the case, committing time and money to a process to improve employee empowerment levels may actually be a waste of time and money.

Organizations should measure employee empowerment levels prior to implementing any new programs. If empowerment levels are in fact low, new programs may be warranted. However, it may be the case that employee empowerment programs are needed in only a few departments. Finding out this information prior to planning any employee empowerment programs will help to ensure dollars and time are used efficiently and effectively.

Counter Productive

Imposing new policies or programs on employees who already have a high level of empowerment may actually be counterproductive. The level of empowerment an employee feels can be very sensitive to changes in an organization. In fact, changing an organization or department in which employees already have high levels of empowerment may actually lower employee feelings of empowerment.

Organizations should be extremely cautious about implementing employee empowerment programs when measurement reveals high levels of employee empowerment. Employees feel empowered for one or more reasons. If an organization happens to change or alter the circumstances that have allowed employees to feel empowered, then employee empowerment levels may fall.

Conscientious Manager

Managers conscientious enough to take a sincere interest in this book may already have some very empowered employees. One of the key ingredients of empowered employees is having a manager who cares. An empowering effect can result from the attitude and actions of managers who are constantly looking for ways to make things better for their employees. The next step, after finishing this book, is to actually measure employee empowerment levels within your organization.

Myth 11: Employee empowerment must involve participatory management.

Reality

Many managers and consultants have concluded that employee empowerment is just another name for participatory management. While it is true organizations incorporating a participatory management style will be doing many of the things necessary to have empowered employees, participatory management is not enough, nor is it appropriate for all organizations.

Participatory management does not ensure empowered employees

An employee's feeling of empowerment can be enhanced by several means. As was mentioned with Myth 3, enhancing the feeling of empowerment among employees can take place through better communication channels, training programs, encouragement, resources, etc. Allowing employees to participate in the management and decision making process of the organization is just another of these ways.

Managers should be careful not to confuse the idea of employee empowerment and participatory management. While it may be desirable for an organization to have empowered employees, the practice of participatory management may not always be the best method of obtaining this goal.

Participatory management is not appropriate for all organizations and employees

The participatory management approach to empowering employees is not appropriate for all organizations and employees. As has been mentioned earlier, it can be dangerous for an organization to entrust incapable, unwilling, maturing, or immature employees with more authority and responsibility. Managers must be careful whom they allow to become involved with the decision making process of the organization.

Professional and Specialized Employees

Professional and specialized employees require special consideration. Professional and specialized employees are individuals with years of training and a specific area of expertise. Allowing these employees the ability to exercise authority and to have responsibility in the areas of their expertise may be essential to insuring their feeling of empowerment. Many times professional and specialized employees can offer legitimate suggestions as to how an organization or departments within an organization can run more smoothly and effectively. In the case of professional and specialized employees, participatory management techniques can be very effective in the overall employee empowerment process.

Epilogue   Where do we go from here?

Upon the completion of this book, a decision must be made. The information contained within these covers can either be put aside, or it can be used to involve an organization in an exciting and constructive process. If the decision is to do nothing, an organization cannot be expected to change. Without the commitment of at least one individual, it is not possible for the employee empowerment process to be initiated.

However, if the decision is to become an organizational emancipator, then things can change. Organizational emancipators become committed to the process of freeing employees. An organizational emancipator looks for ways to ensure employees are enabled to do the job they were hired to do.

All winners

Employee empowerment is not about winners and losers. When implemented properly, everyone is a winner with the employee empowerment process.

The reward for committing to the employee empowerment process, is in the process itself. When an employee commits to the employee empowerment process, he or she takes a big step toward becoming the employee they always wanted to be. Actualizing one's potential through the employee empowerment process allows every committed employee the chance to be a winner.

Process, not a state

Employee empowerment should be viewed as a process and not a state. After it is started, employee empowerment becomes an ongoing process. The employee empowerment process will be in a constant state of evolution. As new obstacles are revealed, alterations in the program may be required. Managers must realize this and not try to cram an employee empowerment program into a two- or three-week program.

Time and commitment

Getting employees to the top will take time and commitment. Employee empowerment is not necessarily an easy or quick process. Individuals looking to become organizational emancipators must realize this and be ready to make sacrifices for the sake of the employee empowerment process.

However, if an individual is truly willing to commit to the employee empowerment process, they should also know it can be very fulfilling. Being an initiator of a process allowing employees to become what they are capable of becoming can be very exciting.

As this book has revealed, the employee empowerment process is extremely complex. However, using the information contained within these covers, managers should feel confident they are one step closer to implementing a successful employee empowerment program.

Now it is up to you. It is time for you to make a commitment to your organization and employees. It is time to begin working toward maximizing the feeling of empowerment with each and every one of your employees.

"Getting employees to the "top" will take time and commitment."

APPENDIX A   Employee Empowerment is Like an Airplane

Employee empowerment is much like an airplane. Consider the elements necessary to make either of the them fly. There are several interesting parallels. Looking at these parallels may help to shed additional light on the employee empowerment process.

Captain to fly

Both the airplane and the employee empowerment process require a captain if their purpose is to be fulfilled. The captain of the employee empowerment process is the organizational emancipator or the manager in charge of the employee empowerment process. The captain must have control over situations and the confidence to handle any bad weather.

Navigator

"Navigator to ensure heading."

The navigator is in charge of mapping out the course and insuring a proper heading. The navigator on an airplane uses radar and maps, but the navigator of the employee empowerment process must use the employee empowerment measurement tool or some other indicator of progress. The navigator is responsible for keeping the process on track and notifying the captain of any apparent obstacles.

Fuel

"Fuel for energy."

Energy of some sort is necessary for the movement of anything. The movement of an airplane is facilitated by an easily obtained liquid fuel. The energy required for the employee empowerment process is human energy, not necessarily as easy to obtain. It is critical that the employee empowerment process maintain power and momentum. A loss of power during flight could result in the destruction of the process.

Passengers

"Passengers willing to fly."

To be successful, both the airplane and the employee empowerment process require passengers willing to travel. Because there is a cost for traveling by airplane, the air travel industry has developed hundreds of marketing and advertising programs designed to encourage more travelers.

The cost for joining the employee empowerment process is giving up the ways of the past. This may seem rather cheap, but with many employees, old habits are hard to break. Therefore, to encourage participants in the employee empowerment process, campaigns which reveal the benefits of this process may have to be developed.

Flight attendants

"Flight attendants to remove second guessing and doubts."

Once the flight is has begun, it is the job of the flight attendant to make sure the ride is as comfortable as possible. The flight attendant is there to remove any second guessing or doubts about flying.

After employees commit to the empowerment process, it is essential they feel comfortable with the organizational changes taking place. The promised working atmosphere may take time to achieve. It is important that little things don't knock the employee empowerment process off course.

Notes

Introduction

1. Evered, Roger D. and James C. Selman (1989) "Coaching and the Art of Management." *Organizational Dynamics*, Autumn, 16-32.

2. Bennis, Warren (1984) "The Four Competencies of Leadership." *Training and Development Journal*, August, 15-19.

Chapter 1   Employee Empowerment

1. Mayo, Elton (1933) *The Human Problems of an Industrial Civilization*. New York: The Macmillan Company.

2. Powell, Reed M. and John L. Schlacter (1971) "Participative Management: A Panacea?" *Academy of Management Journal*, June, 165-173.

3. Homans, George C. (1950) *The Human Group*. New York: Harcourt, Brace & World, Inc.

4. Herzberg, Fredrick, Bernard Mausner, and Barbara Synderman (1959) *The Motivation to Work*. New York: John Wiley & Sons, Inc.

5. McGregor, Douglas (1960) *The Human Side of Enterprise*. New York: McGraw-Hill Book Company.

6. Kaufman, Steven B. (1991) "Empowerment at Pacific Gas & Electric." *Training*, August, 46-48.

7. "Not Power but Empower" (1988) *Forbes*. May 30, 120-123.

8. Schilder, Jana (1992) "Work Teams Boost Productivity." *Personnel Journal*, February, 67-71.

9. Filipowski, Diane (1992) "How Federal Express Makes Your Package Its Most Important." *Personnel Journal*, February, 40-46.

10. Hillkirk, John (1991) "Workers are the key, top firms find." *USA Today*, October 1, 1-2

11. "Not Power but Empower" (1988) *Forbes*. May 30, 120-123.

12. Melvin, Don (1992) "Even Japanese Study Efficiency At Ford Taurus Plant in Atlanta." *Omaha World-Herald*, February 29, 42.

13. Lawler, Edward E. III and Susan A. Mohrman (1987) "Quality Circles: After the Honeymoon." *Organizational Dynamics*, Spring, 42-54.

14. Schilder, Jana (1992) "Work Teams Boost Productivity." *Personnel Journal*, February, 67-71.

15. Burke, W. (1986) "Leadership as Empowering Others." In S. Srivastra (Ed.) *Executive Power* (51-77). San Francisco: Jossey-Bass.

16. Nadler, P. S. (1988) "Pushing Power Down the Corporate Pyramid." *Bankers Monthly*, Vol. 105, 9.

17. Conger, J. A., & Kanungo, R. N. (1988) "The Empowering Process: Integrating Theory and Practice." *Academy of Management Review*, Vol. 13, 471-482.

18. Berry, L. L., Bennett, D., Brown, C. (1989) *Service Quality: A Profit Strategy for Financial Institutions.* Homewood, Illinois: Dow Jones Irwin.

19. French, J., Raven, B. (1960) "The Basis of Social Power." *Group Dynamics*, 2nd ed., (Ed.) Dorwin Cartwright and A. F. Zander. Evanston, IL: Row Peterson, 607-23.

20. Donnelly, J., Gibson, J., Ivancevich, J., (1990) *Fundamentals of Management, Seventh Edition*. Homewood, IL: Business One Irwin.

Chapter 2 Measuring the Feeling of Empowerment Among Employees

1. Byham, William C. (1988) *Zapp, The Lighting of Empowerment*. New York: Harmony Books

2. Linkemer, B. (1991) "Empowering Employees at the Red Cross." *Training and Development*, August, 49-52.

3. Lawler, E. E. (1986) *High-Involvement Management*. San Francisco: Jossey-Bass.

4. Biesada, A. (1992) "Strategic Benchmarking." *Financial World*, September 29, 30-36.

5. Bennet, Amanda (1992) "Firms Run by Executive Teams Can Reap Rewards, Incur Risks." *The Wall Street Journal*, February 5, B1

Chapter 3   Organizational Emancipation Breaking the Chains

1. Bluestone, Irving (1973) "Worker Participation in Decision Making." *The Humanist*, September-October.

2. Bennis, Warren (1984) "The Four Competencies of Leadership." *Training and Development Journal*, August, 15-19.

3. Byrd, Richard E. (1987) "Corporate Leadership Skills: A New Synthesis." *Organizational Dynamics*, Summer, 34-43.

4. Kets de Vries, Manfred F. R. (1991) "Whatever Happened to the Philosopher-King? The Leader's Addiction to Power." *Journal of Management Studies*, Vol. 28, 339-352.

5. ibid.

6. Byrd, Richard E. (1987) "Corporate Leadership Skills: A New Synthesis." *Organizational Dynamics*, Summer, 34-43.

7. Bennis (1984) op. cit.

8. Blanchard, Ken (1992) "Learning to Listen." *Rural Electrification Magazine*, Vol. 50, 17, 42.

9. Peters Tom (1991) "Get Innovative or Get Dead." *California Management Review*, Winter, 9-23.

10. Fleming, Peter C. (1991) "Empowerment Strengthens the Rock." *Management Review*, December, 34-37.

11. Bennis (1984) op. cit.

12. Evered, Roger D., and James C. Selman (1989) "Coaching and the Art of Management." *Organizational Dynamics*, Autumn, 16-32.

13. Kaufman, Steven B. (1991) "Empowerment at Pacific Gas & Electric." *Training*, August, 46-48.

14. Simmons, John (1990) "Participatory Management: Lessons from the Leaders." *Management Review*, December, 54-58.

Myth 3: Empowering employees always implies giving them power.

1. Filipowski, Diane (1992) "How Federal Express Makes Your Package Its Most Important." *Personnel Journal*, February, 40-46.

2. Bell, Chip R. (1991) "Empowerment is Not a Gift." *Training*, December, 98.

3. "Keeping Key Workers" (1991) *The Wall Street Journal*, November 12, 1

4. Peters Tom (1991) "Get Innovative or Get Dead." *California Management Review*, Winter, 9-23.

Myth 4: A universal empowerment program will lead to an entire organization of highly empowered employees.

1. Maren, Michael (1992) "Win: A Master Motivator Teaches You to Create Superstars." *Success*, April, 36-43.

2. Lawler, Edward E. III and Susan A. Mohrman (1987) "Quality Circles: After the Honeymoon." *Organizational Dynamics*, Spring, 42-54.

3. Schilder, Jana (1992) "Work Teams Boost Productivity." *Personnel Journal*, February, 67-71.

4. Fleming, Peter C. (1991) "Empowerment Strengthens the Rock." *Management Review*, December, 34-37.

Myth 5: Making an organization thinner will result in more highly empowered employees.

1. Zalenznik, Abraham (1990) "The Leadership Gap." *The Executive*, February, 7-22.

2. Weinstein, Harold P. and Michael S. Leibman (1991) "Corporate Scale Down, What Comes Next?" *HRMagzine*, August, 33-37.

3. Matejka, Ken and Bill Presutti (1988) "Rebuilding the Survivor's Loyalty." *Management Decision*, Vol. 26, 56-57.

4. Weinstein, Harold P. and Michael S. Leibman (1991) "Corporate Scale Down, What Comes Next?" *HRMagzine*, August, 33-37.

5. "Keeping Key Workers" (1991) *The Wall Street Journal*, November 12, 1

Myth 6: Empowering Employees is a quick fix for an organization.

1. Simmons, John (1990) "Participatory Management: Lessons From The Leaders." *Management Review*, December, 54-58.

2. Fleming, Peter C. (1991) "Empowerment Strengthens the Rock." *Management Review*, December, 34-37.

3. Peters Tom (1991) "Get Innovative or Get Dead." *California Management Review*, Winter, 9-23.

BIBLIOGRAPHY

Adler, Jerry, Pat Wingert, Lynda Wright, Patrick Houston (1992) "Hey I'm Terrific!" *Newsweek*, February 17, 46-51.

Ashforth, B. E. (1989) "The Experience of Powerlessness." *Organizational Behavior and Human Decision Processes*, Vol. 43, 207-242.

Banner, David K., W. Anthony Kulisch and Newman S. Peery (1992) "Self-managing Work Teams (SMWT) and the Human Resource Function." *Management Decision*, Vol. 30, 40-45.

Bell, Chip R. (1991) "Empowerment is Not a Gift." *Training*, December, 98.

Belmer, K. E. (1990) "Employee Surveys, From Start to Finish." *Training and Development Journal*, Vol. 44, 23-26.

Berry, L. L. (1991) "The power of hands-on leadership." *Services Marketing Today*, September/October, Vol. 7, 1.

Berry, L. L., Bennett, D., Brown, C. (1989) *Service Quality: A Profit Strategy for Financial Institutions.* Homewood, Illinois: Dow Jones Irwin.

Blanchard, Ken (1992) "Learning to Listen." *Rural Electrification Magazine*, Vol. 50, pp. 17, 42.

Blanchard, Ken (1992) "The Dynamics of Change." *Rural Electrification Magazine*, May, 19.

Block, P. (1987) *The Empowered Manager: Positive Political Skills at Work.* San Francisco: Jossey-Bass.

Bluestone, Irving (1973) "Worker Participation in Decision Making." *The Humanist*, September-October.

Belasco, James A. (1991) *Teaching the Elephant to Dance, The Managers Guide to Empowering Change*. New York: Penguin Group

Bennet, Amanda (1992) "Firms Run by Executive Teams Can Reap Rewards, Incur Risks." *The Wall Street Journal*, February 5, B1

Bennis, Warren (1984) "The Four Competencies of Leadership." *Training and Development Journal*, August, 15-19.

Bowen, D. E. & Lawler, E. E. (1992) "The Empowerment of Service Workers: What, Why, How, and When." *Sloan Management Review*, Spring, 31-39.

Brayfield, A. H., Rothe, H. F. (1951) "An Index of Job Satisfaction." *Journal of Applied Psychology*, 35, Oct., 307-311.

Burke, W. (1986) "Leadership as Empowering Others." In S. Srivastra (Ed.) *Executive Power* (51-77). San Francisco: Jossey-Bass.

Byham, William C. (1988) *Zapp, The Lighting of Empowerment*. New York: Harmony Books

Byrd, Richard E. (1987) "Corporate Leadership Skills: A New Synthesis." *Organizational Dynamics*, Summer, 34-43.

Cathcart, J. (1988) "Winning Customer Service." *Management Solutions*, November, 10-17.

Conger, J. A. (1991) "Inspiring others: the language of leadership." *The Executive*, February, 31-45.

Conger, J. A., & Kanungo, R. N. (1988) "The Empowering Process: Integrating Theory and Practice." *Academy of Management Review*, Vol. 13, 471-482.

Cone, J. (1989) "The Empowered Employee." *Training & Development Journal*, June, 97-98.

Crosby, P. B., Patricia Nordby Crosby (1991) "Making Change Happen." *Inside Out*, September, 1-2.

Crosby, P. B. (1979) *Quality is Free.* New York: McGraw-Hill Book Company.

Crossan, Des (1987) "A Company Employee Communications Strategy." *Management Decisions*, Vol. 25, 28-34.

Davis, Keith (1968) "Evolving Models of Organizational Behavior." *Academy of Management Journal*, March, 27-38.

Dickson, J. W. (1985) "Some Correlates of Discretion For Chartered Surveyors." *Journal of Management Studies,* Vol. 22:2, 213-224.

Donnelly, J., Gibson, J., Ivancevich, J., (1990) *Fundamentals of Management, Seventh Edition.* Homewood, IL: Business One Irwin.

Dunham, R. B., Smith, F. J. (1979) *Organizational Surveys, An Internal Assessment of Organizational Health.* Glenview, Illinois: Scott, Foresman and Company.

"Empowerment: Helping People Take Charge" (1988). *Training,* Vol. 25, 63-64.

"Empowering the Corporate Culture" (1989). *Training,* February, 16-17.

Evered, Roger D. and James C. Selman (1989) "Coaching and the Art of Management. *Organizational Dynamics*, Autumn, 16-32.

Fairfield, Roy P., Editor (1974) *Humanizing the Workplace.* New York: Prometheus Books

Faltermayer, Edmund (1992) "Is This Layoff Necessary?" *Fortune*, June 1, 71-86.

Feldman, Daniel C. and Carrie R. Leana (1989) "Managing Layoffs: Experiences as the Challenger Disaster Site and the Pittsburgh Steel Mills." *Organizational Dynamics*, Summer, 52-64.

Filipowski, Diane (1992) "How Federal Express Makes Your Package Its Most Important." *Personnel Journal*, February, 40-46.

Fleming, Peter C. (1991) "Empowerment Strengthens the Rock." *Management Review*, December, 34-37.

French, J., Raven, B. (1960) "The Basis of Social Power." *Group Dynamics*, 2nd ed., (Ed.) Dorwin Cartwright and A. F. Zander. Evanston, IL: Row Peterson, 607-23.

Gibson, Cheryl H. (1991) "A Concept Analysis of Empowerment." *Journal of Advanced Nursing*, Vol. 16, 354-361.

Goman, Carol Kinsey (1991) *The Loyalty Factor*. New York: MasterMedia Limited

Greenberger, D. B., Strasser, S., Cummings, L. L., & Dunham, R. B. (1989) "The Impact of Personal Control on Performance and Satisfaction." *Organizational Behavior and Human Decision Processes,* Vol. 43, 29-51.

Herzberg, Fredrick, Bernard Mausner, and Barbara Synderman (1959) *The Motivation to Work*. New York: John Wiley & Sons, Inc.

Hillkirk, John (1991) "Workers are the key, top firms find." *USA Today*, October 1, 1-2

Hinkin, T. R., & Schriesheim, C. A. (1988) "Power and Influence: The View From Below." *Personnel,* Vol. 65, 47-50.

Homans, George C. (1950) *The Human Group.* New York: Harcourt, Brace & World, Inc.

Hwang, Suein L. (1992) "Xerox Forms New Structure For Business." *The Wall Street Journal,* February 5, B6.

Idson, T. L. (1990) "Establishment Size, Job Satisfaction and the Structure of Work." *Applied Economics,* Vol. 22, 1007-1018.

Kahnweiler, William M. (1991) "A Review of the Participatory Management Literature: Implications for HRD Research and Practice." *Human Resource Development Quarterly,* Vol. 2, 229-250.

Kanungo, R. (1982) *Work Alienation, An Integrative Approach.* New York: Praeger.

Kaufman, Roger (1991) *"Toward Total Quality 'Plus'."* *Training,* December, 50-54.

Kaufman, Steven B. (1991) "Empowerment at Pacific Gas & Electric." *Training,* August, 46-48.

"Keeping Key Workers" (1991) *The Wall Street Journal,* November 12, 1

Kets de Vries, Manfred F. R. (1991) "Whatever Happened to the Philosopher-King? The Leader's Addiction to Power." *Journal of Management Studies,* Vol. 28, 339-352.

Keys, Bernard and Thomas Case (1990) "How to become an influential manager." *Executive Management,* Vol. 4, 38-51.

Kotter, J. (1979) *Power in Management.* New York: AMACOM

Kraiger, K., Billings, R. S., & Isen, A. M. (1989) "The Influence of Positive Affective States on Task Perceptions and Satisfaction." *Organizational Behavior and Human Decision Processes,* Vol. 44, 12-25.

Kregoski, Ronald and Beverly Scott (1982) *Quality Circles.* Chicago: The Dartnell Corporation

Lawler, Edward E. III and Susan A. Mohrman (1987) "Quality Circles: After the Honeymoon." *Organizational Dynamics,* Spring, 42-54.

Lawler, Edward E. III (1986) *High-Involvement Management, Participative Strategies for Improving Organizational Performance.* San Francisco: Jossey-Bass Inc.

Lee, James A. (1971) "Behavioral Theory vs. Reality." *Harvard Business Review,* March-April, 20-28, 157-159.

Macher, K. (1988) "Empowerment and the Bureaucracy." *Training and Development Journal,* Vol. 42, 41-45.

Magjuka, Richard J. and Timothy T. Baldwin (1991) "Designing Team-Based Employee Involvement Programs in a Continuous Improvement Environment: An Empirical Investigation." *Human Resource Development Quarterly,* Vol. 2, 207-221.

Manz, Charles C. (1992) *Mastering Self-Leadership, Empowering Yourself For Personal Excellence.* New Jersey: Prentice Hall

Maren, Michael (1992) "Win: A Master Motivator Teaches You To Create Superstars." *Success,* April, 36-43.

Masterson, Thomas R. and Thomas G. Mara (1969) *Motivating The Underperformer.* American Management Association Management Bulletin

Matejka, Ken and Bill Presutti (1988) "Rebuilding the Survivor's Loyalty." *Management Decision*, Vol. 26, 56-57.

Mayo, Elton (1933) *The Human Problems of an Industrial Civilization*. New York: The Macmillan Company.

McGregor, Douglas (1960) *The Human Side of Enterprise*. New York: McGraw-Hill Book Company.

Melvin, Don (1992) "Even Japanese Study Efficiency At Ford Taurus Plant in Atlanta." *Omaha World-Herald*, February 29, 42.

Miller, D. C. (1970) *Handbook of Research Design and Social Measurement, Second Edition*. New York: David McKay Company, Inc.

Murray, Mike (1992) "Secrets of Much More Effective Coaching." *Boardroom Reports*, August 1, 13-14.

Murray, Mike (1991) "A Modest Proposal for Empowering Employees." *Inside Out*, September, 5.

Nadler, P. S. (1988) "Pushing Power Down the Corporate Pyramid." *Bankers Monthly*, Vol. 105, 9.

Neal, A. G., Seeman, M. (1964) "Organizations and Powerlessness: A Test of the Mediation Hypothesis. *American Sociological Review*, April, 216-226.

Niehouse, O. L. (1986) "Job Satisfaction: How to Motivate Today's Workers." *Supervisory Management*, Vol. 31, 8-11.

"Not Power but Empower" (1988) *Forbes*. May 30, 120-123.

Nunnally, J. C. (1978) *Psychometric Theory, Second Edition*. New York: McGraw-Hill Publishing Company.

Orth, Charles D., Harry E. Wilkinson and Robert C. Benfari (1987) "The Manager's Role as Coach and Mentor." *Organizational Dynamics*, Spring, 66-74.

Osburn, Jack D. (1991) "Invited Reaction: Effective Employee Involvement Programs." *Human Resource Development Quarterly*, Vol. 2, 223-227.

Paulhus, D., Christie, R. (1981) "Spheres of Control: An Interactionist Approach to Assessment of Perceived Control." *Research With the Locus of Control Construct (Vol. 1): Assessment Methods*, 161-188.

Peters, Tom (1991) "Get Innovative or Get Dead." *California Management Review*, Winter, 9-23.

Pfeffer, J. (1981) *Power in Organizations.* Massachusetts: Pitman Publishing Inc.

Powell, Reed M. and John L. Schlacter (1971) "Participative Management: A Panacea?" *Academy of Management Journal*, June, 165-173.

Price, J. L., Mueller, C. W. (1986) *Handbook of Organizational Measurement.* Massachusetts: Pitman Publishing Inc.

Rozek, Michael (1991) "Can You Spot a Peak Performer?" *Personnel Journal*, June, 77-78.

Russo, J. Edward and Paul H. Schoemaker (1992) "Managing Overconfidence." *Sloan Management Review*, Winter, 7-17.

Schilder, Jana (1992) "Work Teams Boost Productivity." *Personnel Journal*, February, 67-71.

Scherer, John & Associates (1991) "Learning at Work." *Inside Out*, Fall, 1

Scherer, John (1991) "The Role of Resistance to Change." *Inside Out*, September, 3

"Schools of Empowerment, A new Kentucky law shifts more decision making power to teachers" (1991). *Training & Development*, July, 7-8.

Schoorman, F. David and Benjamin Schneider, Editors (1988) *Facilitating Work Effectiveness*. Lexington, Massachusetts: Lexington Books

Sedwick, R. C. (1975) *People Motivation and Work*. Washington: College and University Press.

Shepard, J. M. (1971) *Automation and Alienation: A Study of Office and Factory Workers*. Cambridge, Mass.: MIT Press.

Simmons, John (1990) "Participatory Management: Lessons From The Leaders." *Management Review*, December, 54-58.

Sleezer, C. M., & Swanson, R. A., (1992). "Culture Surveys." *Management Decision*, Vol. 30, 22-29.

Srivastra, S., & Associates (1986) *Executive Power*. San Francisco: Jossey-Bass.

Stershic, S. F. (1990) "The Flip Side of Customer Satisfaction Research (You Know How Your Customers Feel, But Have You Talked to Your Employees Lately?." *Marketing Research*, Dec., 45-50.

Stewart, Thomas A. (1992) "The Search For The Organization of Tomorrow." *Fortune*, May 18, 92-98.

Tannenbaum, Robert and Warren H. Schmidt (1958) "How to Choose a Leadership Pattern." *Harvard Business Review*, March-April, 115-121.

Tyndall, G. (1990) "How You Apply Benchmarking Makes All the Difference." *Marketing News*, November 12, 18-19.

Weinstein, Harold P. and Michael S. Leibman (1991) "Corporate Scale Down, What Comes Next?" *HRMagzine*, August, 33-37.

Wooten, W. (1991) "The Effects of Self-Efficacy on Job Acceptance Behavior Among American College Students." *Journal of Employment Counseling*, June, 41-48.

Zalenznik, Abraham (1990) "The Leadership Gap." *The Executive*, February, 7-22.

Zemke, R. (1990) "Keeping the Momentum." *The Service Edge*, Vol. 3, 1-7.

About the Author

Allen J. Klose is a nationally recognized business and research consultant. Mr. Klose is currently employed by **BLOCKBUSTER Entertainment Corporation** in Ft. Lauderdale, Florida. Before this, Mr. Klose worked as a management consultant for NRECA Market Research where he worked on over 500 consumer, business and employee research studies.

Mr. Klose has published articles in several academic and trade publications including, *Psychology & Marketing*, *The Journal of Services Marketing*, *Journal of the Market Research Society*, *Journal of International Marketing and Market Research*, *Journal of Business and Entrepreneurship*, *Management Quarterly* and *Marketing News*.

Mr. Klose has earned a MA is Business (Marketing) from the University of Nebraska, Lincoln, a MA in Economics from the University of California, Santa Barbara, and a BA in Economics and Philosophy from Augustana College, in Sioux Falls, South Dakota.

Mr. Klose is available for speaking engagements and can be reached through BLOCKBUSTER Entertainment Corporation.

Any comments can be addressed to the author.

> Allen J. Klose
> P.O. Box 1624
> Ft. Lauderdale, FL 33302-1624